P9-AON-991

"Craig's passion for the backwoods and his wilderness survival experience shine through in his latest book."

—DARRELL BRIMBERRY, US Army Colonel (Retired) and 2018 Appalachian Trail Through-Hiker

ESSENTIAL
WILDERNESS
NAVIGATION

A Real-World Guide to Finding Your Way Safely in the Woods
With or Without a Map, Compass or GPS

CRAIG CAUDILL

Author of *Ultimate Wilderness Gear*, Founder of Nature Reliance School

TRACY TRIMBLE

Navigation Instructor at Nature Reliance School

PAGE STREET
PUBLISHING CO.

PAGE STREET
PUBLISHING CO.

Copyright © 2019 by Craig Caudill and Tracy Trimble

First published in 2019 by
Page Street Publishing Co.
27 Congress Street, Suite 105
Salem, MA 01970
www.pagestreetpublishing.com

Distributed by Macmillan, sales in Canada by The Canadian Manda Group.

24 23 22 21 20   2 3 4 5 6

ISBN-13: 978-1-62414-719-7
ISBN-10: 1-62414-719-4

Library of Congress Control Number: 2018961815

Cover and book design by Meg Baskis for Page Street Publishing Co.
Photography by Jennifer Caudill
Illustrations by Robert Brandt
Maps courtesy of USGS

Printed and bound in China

THIS BOOK IS DEDICATED TO
THE STUDENTS OF NATURE
RELIANCE SCHOOL.

THANK YOU FOR JOINING US
AROUND THE CAMPFIRE.

CONTENTS

INTRODUCTION

I have an important question for you. Would you like to become the next tasty dinner for a pack of wolves? No? Our ancient ancestors felt the same way, and that is why they began using the sky, the landscape and their memory to help them navigate around dangers in the world in which they lived. That danger might have been a pack of wolves on the western side of a mountain or an impenetrable thicket of tangled briars on the south side of a forest. Even though they may not have understood what we call "west" or "south," they did understand direction as it related to their being in the world. They used the sun, stars and various landmarks to help them navigate and survive.

In many ways, we have advanced way beyond our ancient ancestors, and in others, we have fallen far behind them. We have more tools: compasses, global positioning systems (GPS), maps and protractors. We have near-instant messaging through calls and texts, which allows us to communicate more effectively with others we are working or adventuring with. These advancements give us a better understanding of the four cardinal directions and how they relate to the world and us; however, that has now led us to be dependent on such tools in lieu of staying situationally aware of our surroundings. Park rangers throughout the world now commonly use the phrase "death by GPS." This phrase has come to represent those who are tied to technology without the requisite understanding of how and why it works. That reliance has led to many tragedies in the wilderness.

The book you hold in your hands is here to change that. Wilderness navigation is like assembling a puzzle: The more pieces you assemble on a puzzle, the clearer the picture becomes. There are many pieces to the puzzle of wilderness navigation. Maps, compasses, GPS, nature, working solo and with others. What we will be doing with you here is twofold. First, we will ensure that each puzzle piece is clear and understandable. Second, we will teach you how to put it all together.

To that end, you need good teachers to help you "navigate" through the terms, ways and methods of wilderness navigation. This book is a natural transition after my (Craig's) first two books (*Extreme Wilderness Survival* and *Ultimate Wilderness Gear*). Although this book is a natural outgrowth of my previous work, I knew I could not do this one alone. I have enlisted my good friend and fellow Nature Reliance School instructor, Mr. Tracy Trimble, to assist in that endeavor. Tracy was introduced to land navigation in the United States Army Reserve. He now uses these skills on a regular basis while serving as an active search-and-rescue (SAR) team member. He and I have taught backcountry skills to hundreds of people. Each of us brings decades of outdoor experience and, more importantly, tireless hours of study and research into how best to train and teach others.

Most important to us is this: You need to find the information about wilderness navigation relatable and easy to retain. We have taken great pains to take the science of wilderness navigation and distill it down to usable knowledge communicated in everyday language. As one good teacher of ours, Mr. Cornelius Nash, puts it, "There comes a point where the science, and/or the understanding of that science, becomes moot." There are many good books on the topic of wilderness navigation; however, many of our students have told us that the current books available on this topic are hard to read and therefore make it difficult to grasp the information. Our goal with this book was to make it easy to read and use so you can dive into learning. You will be able to learn from this book no matter what your level of training. We have included short quizzes at the end of each chapter to help you see firsthand whether you have retained the important information.

The fundamentals of wilderness navigation are the same, but how we put them into practice varies. We have included sections for a range of uses so that day hikers, through-hikers, hunters, first responders, Boy Scouts, Girl Scouts and many more adventurers can find specific ways to use wilderness navigation.

This all serves to help get you outside practicing skills. Practical application of wilderness navigation skills is imperative to being able to own this skill set. You needed another excuse to go play in the mountains, hills and woods, didn't you?

As with all good manuals, this one has a central focus: to get you outside more. But we want you to get home safely. By mastering the skills presented in this book, you can make time to go outside safely again and again.

As we say at Nature Reliance School: Come on, join in, let's learn together!

THE ESSENTIALS OF WILDERNESS NAVIGATION

By the end of this section, you will be navigating like a champ. First, we will build an excellent foundation on the mind-set, skills, tactics and methods of wilderness navigation. At the end of each chapter, I will give you the key to troubleshooting the common problems that Tracy and I have encountered after decades of navigation experience and of teaching hundreds of students. Then you will find a few questions to verify that you understood the important points of the chapter. Many of these questions will require you to use the enclosed map at the back of the book to test your knowledge practically. I then take you through some practical training methods you can do at home. You will be okay at the skills if all you do is read through the book. You will be much better if you perform the practical exercises. Some of those you will apply in wild places around you; for others, you will use the enclosed map wherever you want to study.

CHAPTER 1

CHOOSING THE RIGHT MAPS AND LEARNING TO READ THEM

It is only the scholar who appreciates that all history consists of successive excursions from a single starting-point, to which man returns again and again to organize yet another search for a durable scale of values. It is only the scholar who understands why the raw wilderness gives definition and meaning to the human enterprise. —Aldo Leopold

As an educator of nearly all things outdoors, I don't think there is anything more tragic than someone dying in a wilderness setting. Especially when the person had gone to the wilderness to take pleasure in a relatively safe adventure. Unfortunately, that is exactly what happened to sixty-six-year-old Geraldine Largay in the summer of 2013. Largay had already hiked more than 1,000 miles (1,600 km) of the famed Appalachian Trail. By all accounts from family and those who hiked and camped with her, she was having a great time and doing very well. Largay was mindful and appreciative enough of the wilderness she loved, that she departed the trail at one point to use the bathroom. (Typical trail etiquette suggests that hikers should move approximately 200 feet (60 m) off the trail when using the bathroom for privacy and to not offend other hikers.)

Largay had been keeping a journal, and it is evident from her entries that she got lost trying to find her way back to the trail after using the bathroom. Upon getting lost, Largay sent several text messages to her husband, asking him to contact authorities for help. Even though she hiked to higher ground for better reception, her texts were never sent due to poor cell connection. Previously, she had normal check-ins and the family knew something was not right when she missed the window of time for those. A massive search-and-rescue (SAR) operation that lasted several weeks did not turn up any conclusive evidence of her whereabouts and was eventually concluded. This fact did not stop wilderness enthusiasts from continuing to search for her when they were in the area. Her journal entries suggest that she actually lived for approximately twenty-six days after she left the trail. She eventually succumbed to a combination of exposure, dehydration and starvation. Her body was found two years later inside of her sleeping bag.

There is much to learn from this incredibly sad story. The first lesson is to enjoy life to the fullest much like Geraldine Largay did. She had earned the trail name "Inchworm" because she was a tad slower than some that passed her while hiking the trail. However, she was out there, hiking more than 1,000 miles (1,600 km) and immensely enjoying herself along the way. Much like other educators, I have read many accounts of her story and feel confident in saying that her tragic experience is not one to keep others from similar adventuring. She would not have wanted that. If anything, she would have wanted—and I want—to ensure that you spend more time outside. By utilizing wilderness navigation skills and tools, I can help you go out and come back home safely. I am not unlike Geraldine Largay in that I love the outdoors, and when I was a young teenager, I, too, got lost in a wilderness setting (though for only a day). It was at that point that I started studying backcountry skills in earnest to ensure that it never happened to me again. My Nature Reliance School was started and my books (including this one) were written to share these skills with others.

In this chapter, I want to lay a good foundation for you to utilize a map effectively. At the end of this and other chapters, you will find two things that will help you develop your own skill set. One is a set of important questions that pull out essential points you need to know about each chapter's topic. You will also find at the end of this chapter (and several others) a section called "Get Out and Practice." Within this section are step-by-step suggestions on how you can develop wilderness navigation methods on your own. This particular chapter has some recommendations to help you avoid falling victim to the situation faced by Geraldine Largay.

In my opinion, maps are the foundation for navigation. Twenty years ago, if you wanted to go hiking or camping and you needed a map, you went to the local forestry service office and purchased a topographic (topo) map of the area. These maps were standard, and you had no real choices in the type, style or options. Today, with the availability of computer software, online services and phone apps, the average hiker has many options to choose from and it can be confusing. So it is critical that the hiker familiarize themselves with these options and gain an understanding of which option is best for them.

Within my favorite map phone app, there are seven different layers to choose from. Each map layer provides different data with its own value depending on my needs. This is one of many indicators in today's world that an outdoor adventurer simply cannot pick up a map and expect it to provide everything that is needed. Most of the time when I go hiking, I will have this same map in at least two different forms. I will always carry a quality paper topography version of the map I need. My second map could be a simple Google Maps overlay, a forestry service trail map or even a local hand-drawn map.

And yes, GPS and phone apps provide maps for the hiker in today's world. Some online mapping services and phone apps only give you a couple options with more options available through paid subscriptions. But these devices often provide a limited view of the area due to small screen sizes. A large printed map will provide you with a much broader overview of the area, offering opportunities for preplanning, setting a supply schedule and a slew of other options.

Selecting the proper map is critical. Please don't think that you can grab your phone or GPS and have all the data—or the best data—you need.

MAPS: UNDERSTANDING YOUR OPTIONS

In my second book, *Ultimate Wilderness Gear*, I stated that if I had to choose between taking a map or a compass to the wilderness, I would take a map. A map can give insight into an area before you get to it and while you are in it, and it can help you do a good after-action review once you return home. Maps are indispensable pieces of equipment. The three-dimensional natural world is a beautiful and diverse place. It takes a heaping amount of symbology, coloration and keys to represent it on a two-dimensional surface that we can put in our pocket. There is so much information that it can easily boggle the mind. So, in this section, we want to unboggle the mind on all those map details.

Our first consideration must be maps in general. In this section, I am only going to cover paper or similar map options. Software, apps and other similar tools will be covered in chapter 3. There are several categories to consider:

- **United States Geological Survey (USGS) quadrangle maps (see image 2):** These are the "gold standard" of maps. All other map options available are either based on these maps, or they utilize the standards of symbology that were formulated for them. Often referred to as "quads," each of these maps have a 1:24000 scale (more on scale later) and will cover approximately 50 square miles (129 sq. km) of land (how much land exactly is determined by its latitude). These maps are standardized in what content they offer. This means that no matter where you are, if you pick up a USGS quad map, you will instantly recognize the symbols, colors and other information contained therein.

- **Large-scale recreational trail maps:** These are instantly recognizable. If you go into any local outdoor store, national park or state park, they will have some sort of recreational trail map. Depending on the area in which you are adventuring, the map may have lots of detail on it or very little detail on it as it relates to topography. For sights to see and points of local interest, this type of map is very useful. Most consider these "starter" maps. They are intended to help a user stay on approved trails and not deviate from them. Most of these maps do not have any way of plotting or determining coordinates. A recreational map should not be your primary map and should be used only for a general overview of the area.

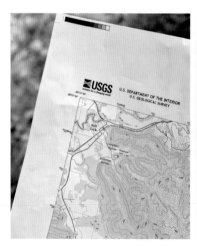

Image 2: The USGS quadrangle maps are the gold standard of maps.

Image 3: Many long trails such as the Sheltowee Trace, Appalachian Trail and others have dedicated guidebooks.

- **Trail guides:** These would most often be classified as small books. They come in two forms. One is a guide for long trails that are either section-hiked or through-hiked. An example is the trail guide for the Sheltowee Trace (see image 3). The Sheltowee Trace is designated as a National Recreation Trail by the US Forest Service, and it travels almost 300 miles (480 km) through beautiful mixed hardwood forests in my home state of Kentucky. The trail guide covers several important features, such as trail profiles, mile markers and good sources of water. Hikers will find this sort of guide a must-have document for multiday hikes on well-known trails, such as the Appalachian or Pacific Crest trails. The second type of trail guide is one that contains multiple short-trail hikes of an area. You can use this type of guide much like a menu. You may ask yourself, "What sort of hike do I feel like doing today?" This type of guide will break down hikes based on distance, points of interest, elevation and difficulty. It allows you to pick the perfect trail to saunter on no matter what level of difficulty you or the group you are with are capable of.

- **Orienteering maps:** For many years, there have been competitions in the practice and use of map and compass skills. These competitions are referred to as orienteering. They are fantastic ways for you to get outside and test your navigation skills. Organizers develop maps, like recreation trail maps, that are used in orienteering competitions and practice. These maps are designed specifically for these competitions, so some of them will purposely leave information off for the sake of training and problem solving. Although they are the perfect maps for this sort of training, they are not good choices for wilderness adventuring. You will want to have as much information as possible on your map when going out.

Now that we have a basic understanding of the types of maps out there, an important question arises: What do we do with it? You will note that chapters 9, 10 and 11 are dedicated to various areas of wilderness interest. In those chapters, I will dig into the details for each specific use. In the following chapters, though, we are going to take you through the important items to observe on a map.

DELORME ATLAS AND GAZETTEER STATE TOPOGRAPHIC MAPS (IMAGE 4)

DeLorme Atlas and Gazetteer provides topographic maps of each of the United States in a large, handy book form. This type of reference tool is an excellent item to keep in your vehicle. You can use it to relate the information from your vehicle GPS device (such as a TomTom, Google Maps or Apple Maps) directly to a paper map. This reference tool also provides you with a backup tool when you experience a problem with your GPS receiver. If you are in an unfamiliar area and your GPS takes you to a closed road and reroutes you, you can then verify the area you are going into with the Gazetteer.

Image 4: DeLorme's Gazetteer or a Road Atlas (right) are must-have backup resources to keep in your vehicle.

DATUM SET

In wilderness navigation, if you are communicating with others or deciphering your position, you can easily be off by hundreds of meters if you don't understand how to use datum sets. Datum are essentially a set of rules that help us apply grid systems to the earth. This facilitates communication between us and others about positions, places and more. The following are those of importance in the United States:

- **North American Datum Set of 1927 (NAD 27):** This is the system you will find on older topo maps. It was designed using transit surveying methods.

- **North American Datum Set of 1983 (NAD 83):** This is a system similar to NAD27 that was updated utilizing global positioning satellites and allowed datum to be inherently more accurate.

Produced by the United States Geological Survey
North American Datum of 1983 (NAD83)
World Geodetic System of 1984 (WGS84). Projection and
1 000-meter grid: Universal Transverse Mercator, Zone 17S
10 000-foot ticks: Kentucky Coordinate System of 1983 (north zone)

This map is not a legal document. Boundaries may be generalized for this map scale. Private lands within government reservations may not be shown. Obtain permission before entering private lands.
Imagery..NAIP, June 2014
Roads.....................................U.S. Census Bureau, 2014 · 2015
Roads within US Forest Service Lands............FSTopo Data with limited Forest Service updates, 2012 · 2015
Names...GNIS, 2015
Hydrography....................National Hydrography Dataset, 2014
Contours...........................National Elevation Dataset, 2002
Boundaries............Multiple sources; see metadata file 1972 · 2015

Wetlands.........FWS National Wetlands Inventory 1977 · 2014

- **World Geodetic System of 1984 (WGS 84):** This is the same datum put together for NAD83 but applied on a worldwide scale, not just in the United States.

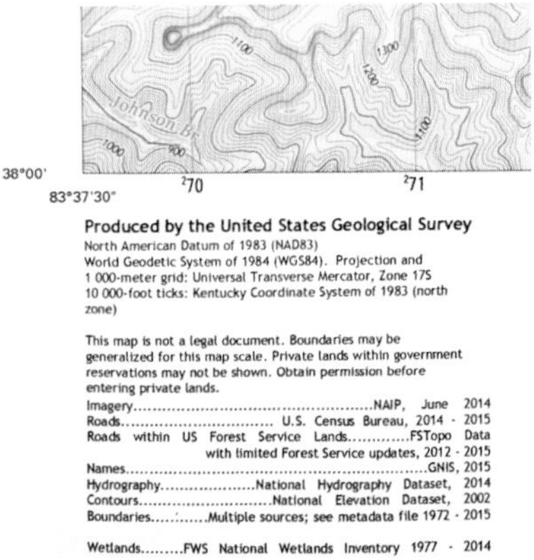

Image 5: The datum sets can be found on the lower-left corner of USGS quadrangle maps.

- **North American Terrestrial Reference Frame of 2022 (NATRF 2022):** This is the future of land navigation map datum. This new system is being put in place so that all of North America (Canada, United States and Mexico) are on the same datum reference.

One of the first things you should do when looking at any map for the first time is take note what datum set it references. This is vitally important if any of the following are true:

- You are using a GPS. If your GPS is set on one datum and the map you are referencing is another, you could be several hundred meters off.

- You are communicating with another person or party for a current trip or one in the future. You and the other party will most likely reference various coordinates. If you are using different datum sets, these locations will be different (see image 5).

- You are a first responder and work with other agencies. For example, if a police agency gets a 911 call of coordinates for a location, a search-and-rescue team would benefit greatly by knowing what datum was used so they can narrow their search.

SCALE

The scale of the map is the amount the map has been reduced from the actual portion of the earth it represents. Typically, this is found in one of the lower corners of a map. On USGS quad maps, it is always found in the bottom center. In image 6, you will note the scale of this USGS quad map is labeled as 1:24000. This means that 1 unit on the map is equal to 24,000 of those same units on the earth. For example, if you measure between two points of interest on a map and that distance is 1 inch (2.5 cm), the distance on the actual ground, if you were to walk between them, would be 24,000 inches (60,000 cm). This equates to 2,000 feet (610 m) or slightly over ⅓ mile (530 m). This is one of the most vital pieces of information you can get from a map, and it has pros and cons. Positively, a map allows us to carry around a representation of the earth in our pocket without much trouble. Negatively, if we do not pay close attention to our map's scale, then it is more difficult to translate what we are seeing on our map to what we are seeing on the ground in front of us. Looking at the scale of the map is therefore critical to wilderness navigation.

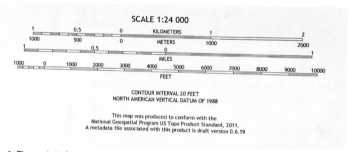

Image 6: The scale is found in the center of the bottom legend of USGS quadrangle maps.

METRIC VERSUS IMPERIAL MEASUREMENTS

You will find that this text will share both Imperial and metric measurements throughout. It is our observation that beginners understand metric measurement much easier than standard measurement. The following two equations and a bit of history can illustrate this point:

1 kilometer = 1,000 meters; 1 meter = 100 centimeters

1 mile = 5,280 feet; 1 foot = 12 inches

Why is the Imperial (aka customary) form of measurement so confusing? The word "mile" is derived from the Latin term *mille passus*, which translates as "1,000 paces." That was considered the original Roman mile. Despite the often larger-than-life persona that is attributed to Roman soldiers, history has shown that during that time, their mile was approximately 4,840 feet (1.5 km). This means the average stride length (a measurement of left foot to left foot) was 5 feet (1.5 m). This is slightly less than our average stride length today. In more modern times, our larger stride length means that 1,000 paces will take us 5,280 feet (1.77 km).

COLORS

The colors on a map are very beneficial. They give us a quick reference to what is on the earth. Please reference image 7; this graphic shows us the colors primarily used on USGS maps. Please note that although USGS maps are the "gold standard," recreation, private and other similar maps are not required to utilize this same color scheme. Most of them do, but it is important to look at the legend and verify this before you make decisions based on that information. This is another reason that we are proponents of using maps in which standards are the same as the USGS. This allows us to quickly and efficiently use maps of that caliber. There are a few colors that seem to work well across all maps, no matter what their origin:

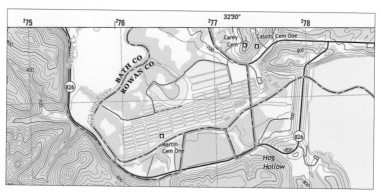

Image 7: There is a wide range of colors on any map. Use the appendix in the back of this book to decipher them.

- **Green:** Forested or wilderness landscape.

- **White:** Sparse or no vegetation (including but not limited to urban areas).

- **Blue:** Waterways or bodies of water.

- **Brown:** Topography lines (see the section titled "Contour Lines" on page 31).

- **Black:** Man-made objects.

- **Purple:** Revisions that have been made to a map using aerial photos.

For emphasis: The preceding colors are not true for all maps, although this is true for all quality maps like USGS quad maps.

SYMBOLOGY

The symbology that you find on a map is intuitive enough that most items on the map or in the legend will be easy to understand. Please review the appendix starting on page 261 for a detailed look at a publication put out by the USGS entitled "Topographic Map Symbols." For those interested in the serious use of maps for engineering, surveying, real estate and other similar interests, knowing these symbols will be part of the job. For those of us interested in

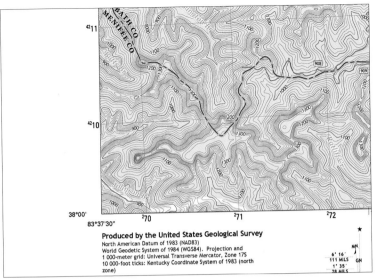

Image 8: Recognizing boundary lines on maps is a must-have skill to keep you safe and in the correct area.

wilderness adventure, we will typically come across only a smattering of them. In this section, I want to highlight a few that will be representative of others on a map. Please keep in mind that recreation and trail maps will have their own symbology but will often mimic what you see here. The following are several important reasons for studying map symbology:

• Understanding the boundaries (see image 8) of an area is vitally important. For example, understanding boundaries will prevent you from wandering away from national forestland.

• Waterways are important features to determine on extended hikes and are good choices for terrain association on any hike. By knowing where waterways are, you can save the trouble of carrying too much water—with knowledge of their locations, you can plan on filtering water. Rivers and long streams are also easily recognizable features in the topography and easy to translate what you are seeing on your map to what you see in front of you on the earth.

- Knowing the symbols for man-made objects allows you to travel in a "gross direction" for self-rescue when you are potentially lost. Some possible objects are cell towers and right-of-ways for utilities.

- Improved and unimproved roads, trails and other related features are the primary sources for travel in the wilderness for most. In the event you are a new visitor to an area and you get lost, being able to navigate to one of these will bring you home. (I will teach you how to do this later in the book.)

- Utility right-of-ways are found virtually everywhere now. They are often kept cleared and are easy for a beginner to the outdoors to identify. This, in turn, helps the person associate their position on the map to the earth and vice versa.

ORIENTING YOUR MAP

Orienting a map is very simple, but this process is incredibly important to the use of the map in the field. When you orient a map, you place it in your hands, on the ground or on a notebook in such a way that the four cardinal directions (north, south, east and west) on the map correspond to your actual position on the earth. This is done by understanding where north is on the earth and using your map so that north points in the same direction.

Knowing where north is should be a skill you develop each day. One way to do this is to use your compass. We will go into detail on this in the next chapter. For now, suffice it to say nearly everyone knows how to use a compass to find north. Use the north-seeking arrow of your compass to find north. Once it is found, lay the edge of your compass along the borderline of your map. Turn the map and compass as a unit until you are facing north as indicated on the compass (this will be covered in chapter 2 under the sidebar entitled "Who is Red Fred and Why is He in a Shed?," page 54). By doing this, your map is oriented to north as well.

Locating north can cause confusion when you are using an app or mapping software. In some programs, the arrow will always point north, but the map will adjust based on the user's positioning. On the map there will be an actual arrow or numerical indicator of north. If you are using software, especially on a GPS or handheld device, make certain you know which portion is north by referencing the arrow.

GRID LINES AND TICK MARKS

On USGS maps, you will notice that on the outermost edge there are tick marks, which indicate where grid lines would start and end without covering the whole map. You can often find other digital and printed maps that will have an actual grid that covers the map. These grid lines are there to help pinpoint the grid coordinates that are found on a map. Grids are very similar to datum sets in that they are there for quantifying locations on a map. This allows people to communicate effectively and efficiently about various points and to also help measure the distance from one point to another. Please note that on the map we have provided you with this book, the gridlines have been placed and are covering the whole map. There are a few different grid systems in regular use today:

- **Universal Transverse Mercator (UTM):** This is a metric-based system commonly used by search-and-rescue personnel.

- **United States National Grid (USNG):** This is a metric-based system that more modern first responders, including the Federal Emergency Management Agency and search-and-rescue teams, are starting to use.

- **Military Grid Reference System (MGRS):** This is a metric-based system used by the United States military.

- **Latitude and Longitude (Lat/Long):** This is the oldest known method for map grids available. It is still heavily used by pilots of ships and aircraft.

Even though you will regularly see the four preceding grid systems in use today, the first three have only slight differences. USNG and MGRS are both based on the UTM system. We recommend starting with UTM because it is the most widely used. If you spend time learning UTM, you will in effect learn the others as well. The following section, and the table that follows it, will help you to understand why.

When looking at grid coordinates, there are several pieces of information that you need to break it into sections for the sake of understanding. When you look at these coordinates, you are looking at four or five pieces of information; each one is vital to understanding the location.

READ RIGHT, THEN UP

One of the key components of noting coordinates for yourself or sharing with others is to not get the coordinates for easting or northing switched. One simple method that we have utilized to teach this is to tell our students to always read right first, then up. This allows them to note the coordinates in order properly.

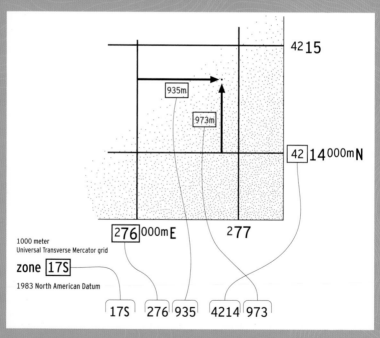

Image 9: This illustration represents how to recognize the different parts of UTM (and other) metric coordinate systems. Many thanks to maptools.com for their training insight.

As an example, let's use the following UTM coordinates to help us understand what all these numbers mean (you can also reference image 9 to understand this more clearly): **17S 0276935 4214973**

- **Zone:** This is the two-digit numeric designator on the left of the string of digits. In our example, the zone is 17.

- **Lateral band:** This is the alpha (i.e., letter) designator to the right of the zone. In our example, the lateral band is S.

- **Easting:** This is the first set of numbers. This represents the easterly position within that grid zone. In our example, the easting number is 0276935.

- **Northing:** This is the second set of numbers. This represents the northerly position within that grid zone. In our example, the northing number is 4214973.

Even within the various metric grid systems, there is some variance on how the coordinates are designated—we created the following table to help you understand the differences. The coordinates listed here are all the same location. Please note that USNG and MGRS are slightly different than UTM. The first two digits of UTM coordinates indicate the 100,000 square identifier. The USNG and MGRS use an alpha designator to identify this. In our table, you will note how they replace numeric designators.

Tater Knob Tower Bath County, Kentucky	Zone	Lateral Band	Alpha Designator	Easting	Northing	Shared
UTM	17	S		0276935	4214973	17S 0276935 4214973
USNG	17	S	KC	76935	14973	17S KC 76935 14973
MGRS	17	S	KC	76935	14973	17SKC7693514973

Each of the columns represents the various pieces of information that are important to understanding these metric grid systems. The last column, entitled "Shared," contains the way the information will be shared with others and how the coordinates should be written down. You will note there are no breaks for MGRS. It is vital that you have good communication skills when sending or receiving these coordinates with others—especially as it pertains to radio or phone transmission. We detail this in chapter 3.

The latitude and longitude system used worldwide is accurate but is more difficult for the average adventurer to utilize. Most GPS receivers default to latitude and longitude (see image 10). If you have a handheld device that makes the calculations for you, this is not an issue, but once you run out of battery and you need to determine distances or locations visually on a map, you will have difficulty. To better understand just what latitude and longitude are, consult the following explanations:

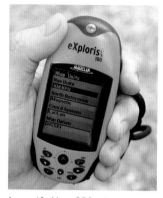

Image 10: Most GPS units are defaulted to latitude and longitude.

• **Latitude:** These are the horizontal parallel lines used to measure the distance between the two poles. The equator is designated as 0 degrees and the North and South Poles are defined as 90 degrees. These lines are often referred to as parallels.

• **Longitude:** These lines are not parallel and converge on the North and South Poles. They are used to measure the east-to-west position. The starting point for these lines, called the prime meridian, runs directly through Greenwich, England. If you go east of the prime meridian, you will measure in degrees east. This is considered a positive number and identified with a + sign or no sign at all. If you go west of the prime meridian, you will measure in degrees west. This is considered a negative number and identified with a - sign.

The coordinates that follow list the latitude and longitude of the same location we utilized in the previous detailing of metric grid systems:

38°03'18.3600" -83°32'33.7200

You can see it uses the positive-negative notation (usually the "+" sign is understood) and not *east* or *west*. A west, or "-" designation, means the longitude is west of the prime meridian. They can be used interchangeably. For example, the following coordinates are the same, just noted differently:

38°03'18.3600"	-083°32'33.7200"
38°03'18.3600"N	083°32'33.7200"W

There are also other ways to format the same coordinate, shown in the following table.

Tater Knob Tower Bath County, Kentucky	Latitude	Longitude
Degrees, Minutes, Seconds	38°03'18.3600"	-083°32'33.7200"
Degrees and Decimal Minutes	38°03.30600	-083°32.56200
Decimal Degrees	38.0551000°	-083.5427000°

As you study the preceding table, remember the following definitions:

- **Degrees, minutes, seconds:** This is the most commonly found format in use on maps. You must think of this in the same way you think of time. Where 60 seconds = 1 minute, 60 minutes = 1 degree. We understand this can be confusing, because it is. It is also why we nearly exclusively teach by utilizing a metric-based system, such as UTM, USNG or MGRS. Utilizing Lat/Long is a process of memorization in which you are required to memorize the degrees, minutes and seconds equation.

- **Degrees and decimal minutes:** This is the most commonly used format for electronic navigation equipment such as GPS receivers and equipment in aircraft and boats.

- **Decimal degrees:** This is the most common system for online and computer-based systems. For example, this is the default setting for Google Maps.

NORTH ARROWS

As we look at the north arrows on your map, you will note that there are often three of them. Understanding these arrows is important to accurate map reading. North arrows are typically found on the bottom center of topography (topo) maps. Topo maps are those that detail the land features of an area.

- **True north:** This is also known as geodetic north (image 13, page 33), geographic north or terrestrial north. It is often represented by a star in the topographic diagrams. It refers to the axis on which the earth rotates. All meridian lines converge at a singular position that we refer to as the North and South Poles.

THE AGONIC LINE

The Agonic Line is the imaginary line that runs from the north magnetic pole to the south magnetic pole all the way around the earth. For those in the United States, it will run through the state of Wisconsin and down through the western side of Florida. It is along this line that declination remains zero. This means that magnetic north and geographic true north are the same. Understanding the Agonic Line is fundamental to understanding the importance of declination, which is covered in the sidebar entitled "Deciphering Declination" on page 32.

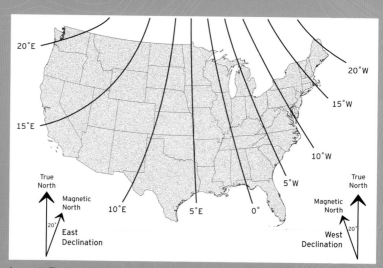

Image 11: The center line in this illustration depicts the Agonic Line, which is where declination is 0°.

- **Magnetic north:** This varies from true north due to the earth's natural magnetic field. On older topographic maps it is indicated by a small flag or what sometimes appears as a pointer on the end of the line. An accurate compass will point to this location. The arrow of your compass that points to the North Pole is commonly referred to as the north-seeking arrow. Magnetic north changes over time, so verify when using maps that you have one that is relatively new. The National Oceanic and Atmospheric Administration's (NOAA's) National Geophysical Data Center will have updated magnetic declination amounts.

- **Grid north:** This allows us to use the UTM grid lines essentially as true north lines. Grid north lines do not deviate more than 2 degrees. This variance is due to transferring the earth's spherical surface to a flat plane surface.

CONTOUR LINES

Contour lines are often referred to as topography, topo or elevation lines. They are often, very informally, referred to as the "brown squiggly lines" that make up the bulk of the information you can see on a map. These are one of the most important features that help us decipher the three-dimensional world on a two-dimensional surface. Cartographers (mapmakers) of old had the challenge of showing mountains, hills, valleys, plains and much more. They determined a good point of reference would be sea level. If it were possible for you to walk along one of these imaginary lines, you would walk along the same exact distance above sea level for the entirety of the line.

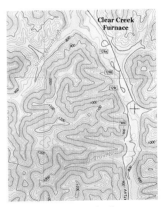

Note that there are some lines that are bolder or darker than the others. These are referred to as index lines. If you look along these lines you will see a number within them. The number you see there is the distance above sea level. Look at image 12, and you will note that two index lines can be seen as 1,000 and 1,100. This means that there are 100 feet (30.5 m) of elevation between those two lines. Since there are five spaces (four lines) between each of those, we can easily determine that there is

Image 12: Contour index lines appear bolder and have the elevation within them. In this graphic, you can see index lines indicating 800, 900, 100, 1100 and 1200.

an elevation change of 20 feet (6 m) between each of those lines. This 20-foot (6-m) change is referred to as the contour interval. Each space represents 20 feet (6 m). This is the standard on nearly all topography. The only variation to this is in areas where the landscape is mostly flat with very little elevation change. This graphic was taken from a map with a 1:24000 scale and is the standard for most USGS maps.

Since the distance between the lines is a direct correlation to change in elevation, it is easy to use the two-dimensional map to help us understand the three-dimensional world that we will be traveling in. For example, the wider apart the lines, the less elevation change, which means this is a flatter area of land. If you see contour lines converging together in one location, you are looking at a cliff line. Those in a flat plain area such as Nebraska will see very few contour lines on a map. In these areas, you will see intermediate contour lines and they will be half the elevation of a standard contour line. Conversely, those of us here in Kentucky have many areas, such as the Red River Gorge, where we will regularly see the contour lines converging on a map, indicating a cliff line. The examples that follow in image 14 are key land features that you can note from contour lines.

DECIPHERING DECLINATION

Declination (also called "magnetic declination" and "variation") is the angle between magnetic north and true north. To make it more understandable, think of it like this: Your compass is pulled away from true north due to the magnetic properties of the earth. To navigate most accurately, you should utilize both a map and a compass; however, each of these gives different information about the direction of north. Your map is a representation of many things, and two of those things are truth north and grid north. Your compass shows many things, and one of those things is magnetic north. Since these norths are different, you must know the difference and account for it based on which of these items you are using.

If you look only at the map, you could go about using only grid north. This is because the grid lines on the map reference this north. But if you want to navigate with a compass, you will need to know the declination amount and make the adjustments necessary. In image 13 you can see that the declination listed as 6 degrees, 16 minutes of angle.

The key thing to know about declination is that it changes based on where you are located on the earth. For example, we teach classes in Wisconsin each year and the declination is virtually zero because it's located along the Agonic Line (see page 30). Any area that is

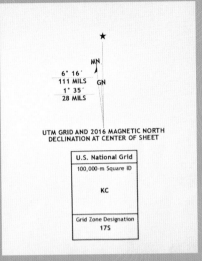

Image 13: Wilderness navigators must know their declination amount to use a map and compass together accurately.

found on the east side of the line has west declination, and what is west of that line has east declination. Yes, please go ahead and read that sentence again. At first, this may seem confusing until you realize that the declination references the direction in which the compass needle is pulled away from geographic north. In the eastern US, the magnetism pulls the needle toward the west. In the west, this same magnetism pulls the needle to the east. This is because the map is a representation of the earth and as such it will show true north. If all we are doing is planning routes or locating waypoints in a stationary location, then gathering the directional heading from the map is simple. If our goal is to navigate by hiking, biking, driving or another mode of transportation, we will need to adjust our compass. This change is declination. You will need to adjust your compass in the field and will need to know what it is before we get to the field.

Image 14: Topography map representing (from top left clockwise) a gentle (walking) slope, a steep hill, a cliff line, the peak of a hill and a saddle.

Here are a few tips to help you gather important information from the contour lines:

- The smallest ring in a grouping of concentric circles is the peak of a hill. It is sometimes marked with an X.

- The V shape of valleys points toward increasing elevation (that is, higher ground).

- U- and V-shaped patterns of contour lines indicate either an area where water erosion has occurred over a short (e.g., a small ravine) to long (e.g., the Grand Canyon) period of time. To distinguish between the two, take note of the elevation changes.

- To determine if a trail is going uphill or downhill, note the elevation changes. Remember, only the index lines are labeled with an amount. You may use those to determine how much change there is on any portion of your map.

- If contour lines were to appear on the earth, you could travel around them and eventually come back to your starting point.

UNDERSTANDING SLOPE GRADIENTS

Since your map is a two-dimensional surface, it is often difficult to grasp how intense or easy traveling up a slope will be. Sometimes building a slope profile is helpful to visualize this. Take, for example, image 15. In this image, you will see a short hike that travels up a slope from point A to point B. Let's take the information available to us and plot it on a graph (image 15). Along the X axis of our graph, we have the linear distance of the hike. Along the Y axis, we have the elevation at different points. As you can tell, this is a rather gently sloping hike—one that could easily be traveled by someone new to hiking or simply wanting an easy stroll in the woods. Compare that with the graph represented in image 15. This graph depicts a hike that is rather easy and will not require use of technical measures or equipment.

Image 15: Map and quick gradient sketch in the field to get a better understanding of a slope.

This image depicts a slope gradient of 1 foot (30.5 cm) in 20 feet (6 m). By drawing this, you can start to get a feel for how hard this hike will be. For example, in this drawing, the slope is rather gentle. Hiking that distance should be a fun and enjoyable walk.

VALLEY, RAVINE, GULLEY, GULCH, ARROYO, HOLLOW, HOLLER: WHICH ONE IS CORRECT?

The Appalachian dialect is dear to the heart of the Kentuckians that are writing this book. In this part of the world, we have areas in which water erosion over hundreds and thousands of years have created a deep cut into the earth. After teaching wilderness navigation skills throughout the country, as well as having students in our classes from around the world, we have discovered there is quite a disparity on what different people call this geographical feature. There is a slight difference and we hope to help translate it for you here:

1. Valley: A valley can be defined as the low area between two hills or mountains, typically containing a stream that runs through it. Areas typically noted as valleys will have gentle or mild slopes leading to the low area for most of their long length.

2. Gorge: This is a deep and narrow area that has steep sides. *Ravine* is another word often utilized for this type of area.

3. Gulley: This is an area that has had recent waterworn erosion. Most users of this term refer to something that is much smaller than a valley or gorge.

4. Gulch: This is an area also eroded by water and may contain a streambed or a dry creekbed. Gulches are typically larger than gulleys but smaller than valleys.

5. Arroyo: This is a word of Spanish origin that means *gulley*. This term is often heard and used in the arid or semiarid regions of the southwestern United States and in Mexico.

6. Hollow: This term literally refers to something that has a hole or empty space inside. Hollow is often used by those in the southeastern United States to mean any valley (big or small) within the Appalachian Mountains.

7. Holler: This is an incredibly common but mispronounced version of the word *hollow*. This term is often used by those who spend the greater portion of their lives in rural or mountainous areas of Appalachia.

RATING SYSTEMS FOR STEEPNESS

Mountaineers, climbers and hikers often need a common language to share information about how steep a travel route is. In North America, the primary system used is called the Yosemite Decimal System. There are five class levels in this system:

1. Class 1: This consists of simple and normal walking paths. Think of a cityscape and how easy it is to walk on. There may be small hills or slopes, but the walking is rather easy. The same class level is utilized for trails of similar make.

2. Class 2: This indicates steep areas that can be found on or off the trail. This is most common in mountainous regions.

3. Class 3: This means there are areas that are steep enough, or ground that is loose enough, that you may need to scramble to move across them. This is common in areas where there are large boulders or loose grade on a steep incline. Scrambling will likely require the use of your hands to move in areas of this class level.

4. Class 4: These are climbs in which ropes are most often utilized. Falls in these types of areas will lead to severe injury or death.

5. Class 5: These are areas where is it most practical to use ropes, belay devices and partners to climb. Rock climbers further divide this classification from 5.0 to 5.15. This rating assists climbers in communicating about routes. Higher levels of difficulty will require more physical and mental stamina as well as various pieces of equipment to assist the climber.

TERRAIN ASSOCIATION

There are many things you can learn by reading a book (thank you for buying this one), and there are some things that will require you to get ample experience to be able to understand them at all. Terrain association is one of those things. Terrain association is the actual field use of your map to orient yourself on the earth. Terrain association is simple to do when you are at the fork of a river that you already know the name of. It is much more difficult when you are looking at a ravine on a map and you have two that are in front of you on the earth.

Topography maps are incredibly accurate. To use them well, you need lots of "dirt time," and you need to pay attention to what appears on the map and what does not. For example, you might be hiking along a trail and see that a small ravine that is being created by a small stream is cutting the trail and coming from the east. You note it on your map and then continue hiking. As you continue, you come across another, much larger ravine and stream intersecting the trail coming from the east; however, there is no second stream on your map. Most likely, the larger stream is the one depicted and the smaller stream is not on the map at all. While this book is an excellent text to get you familiar with hilltops, saddles, ravines and more (as well as how they appear on the map), it cannot replace your going afield with a map of a known area and looking at what an actual saddle looks like in nature rather than what it looks like just on a map. Field practice allows you to transfer that understanding to your mind for later use. In our wilderness navigation course at Nature Reliance School, we spend the last day doing nothing but terrain association, hiking and looking at land features and showing our students where they appear on the map. Take that as an example and spend adequate amounts of time hiking and seeing what items appear—and what items don't appear—on the map.

Using a map is like holding a textbook that can tell you a tremendous amount of information about an area before you ever set foot in it. It is why we recommend that if you take anything at all into a wilderness for navigation purposes, take a map. Couple it with a compass and the skill to use them together and you can navigate anywhere in the world. But before we take a look at compasses, we need to address three very important considerations to help you develop your own skill set. The first is a section on troubleshooting common problems that occur with maps. Second, we have some questions for you to ensure that you grasp the essentials from this chapter. Third, we have a step-by-step way that you can start training now with maps.

TROUBLESHOOTING: OVERCOMING COMMON PROBLEMS WITH YOUR MAPS

Following are some troubleshooting tips for using maps:

FOLDING YOUR MAP

The first problem with maps that should be addressed is the simple way of storing and utilizing them. Most trail maps will come already folded and are easy to put back in place for easy storage and transport. If you purchase USGS topo maps, they will often come rolled. You will want to fold them for wilderness travel. Please see image 16 to see a common method of folding maps. This allows you to keep all your maps together and makes it easy to find the one you are looking for. Just bear in mind that if you have a map that you fold and unfold regularly, it will eventually wear in the folds. The information depicted in the folds will get obscured over time. Be sure to check your maps before you need them in the field; doing so will allow you to see if your maps are developing too many of these problem areas and give you the opportunity to replace them before you go afield.

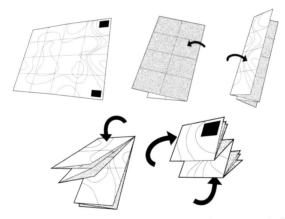

Image 16: The proper way to fold a map so that important information can be found while folded.

39

PROTECTION

Unless you purchase waterproof maps, you will need to do something to protect your maps from regular use and moisture. Rain is an obvious problem, but what is often overlooked is sweat, dew and dirty hands. Murphy's Law can bite us sometimes. If you let one big drop of sweat hit your map, it will eventually obscure that short cliff line you need to be aware of. Map cases are worthwhile investments, but if you don't want to purchase one, you can achieve nearly the same protection by utilizing a large sealable storage bag. Another method is to cover the map in high-quality, durable packing tape before you go outdoors. This has quickly become a go-to method for Nature Reliance School instructors. It also gives us the benefit of writing on the map with a dry-erase marker for instructional purposes. This method will also serve you well if you want to temporarily make marks on your map to determine headings or distances. Dry-erase markers can also be used to make tick marks on the map when utilizing them for terrain association.

MEASUREMENTS

A common problem with using a map is not taking the time to look at the information provided on it. No matter what map you are using, there are a few items you should know about it before you even begin using it:

- **Note the scale of the map.** Pay special attention if you have printed from a software program, online provider or were handed one by a hiking partner. These maps are not always 1:24000 like your standard USGS topo map.

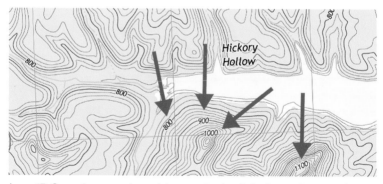

Image 17: Count the contour intervals between the given index lines to determine elevation along each contour line.

- **Note the datum and grid system used on the map.** These should coordinate with those of the people you are adventuring with, as well as your GPS receiver.

- **Note the declination of your area.** You cannot have an accurate transfer from map to compass or compass to map without knowing your declination.

When utilizing a string, stick, cloth or similar item to measure distance on the map, make sure you lay it on the map the same way you put it on the scale. If you stretch the string on the map, then let it lie naturally on the scale, you will not be accurate. This will affect your distance and your pace count. If both of these are off, you could easily miss your destination.

ELEVATION

One common thing that confuses new wilderness navigators on the map is the elevation increase or decrease. We detailed this well earlier in the chapter; however, it bears repeating that elevation change is a simple math equation. Look at the contour lines that appear bold or darker (the index lines). You must first get the total elevation change by subtracting the lower index line elevation from the higher index line elevation. You can then count the number of spaces between the other elevation lines. Divide the amount of total elevation change by that number of spaces. This will give the amount of elevation change between each of those lines. With many of the new software maps, there is not a standardization of contour intervals, so it is vital that you are able to calculate this (see image 17).

QUESTIONS FOR PRACTICE

1. What is the datum for the map enclosed with this book?

2. What is the scale for the map?

3. If I measured 2 inches (5 cm) on the map, how many feet would this be on the earth?

4. Are there clear or open fields identified on this map?

5. What does the circle with the number 211 represent on the map?

6. What do the grid lines on the map represent?

7. Can you use this map for Lat/Long, UTM, USNG and MGRS coordinates?

8. What is the declination value for this map?

9. True or false: Another name for true north is magnetic north.

10. What is the contour interval for this map?

Answers: (1) NAD 83; WGS 84. (2) 1:24000. (3) 4,000 feet (1.2 km). (4) Yes. (5) State Route 211. (6) UTM grid system. (7) Yes. (8) 6 degrees, 16 minutes; 6.27 degrees. (9) False. True north and magnetic north are different points. (10) 20 feet (6 m).

GET OUT AND PRACTICE

Practical application of your skills is the difference between your understanding the skills we have shared thus far and your actually being able to use them. The following is a step-by-step process for you to begin developing wilderness navigation skills by utilizing a map. In the subsequent chapters, we will add more skills to these processes as we learn them.

☐ Determine a location in which you would like to do a short hike. I recommend for your first adventure that you choose a spot that has developed trails. If no trails are available, hike along the road as long as it is safe to do so. This could be a nature sanctuary, national forest or other public-access wilderness.

☐ Once a location is determined, locate their website to see if they have maps available on location. If so, ask how much they are and how and where to obtain one. Even if they offer maps, most of them will be trail maps only with little or no topography on them. You should also choose one of the map providers listed in the appendix of this book. Get a topography map of the area as well.

☐ Look at your map and determine the datum and grid that it uses. If you have multiple maps or are using an app, verify that they match one another.

☐ Look at the scale. For quick reference, lay your finger down on the scale to get an approximation of what portion of your finger represents 1,000 meters (3,280 feet) on your map. Use a straightedge to get an exact representation of what 1,000 meters (3,280 feet) is on your map.

☐ Find a portion of trail that has a straight-line distance on it for approximately 1,000 meters (3,280 feet). Mark the beginning of that as point A. Wherever that straight-line 1,000 meters (3,280 feet) ends, mark as point B.

☐ Draw a slope gradient of this hike from point A to point B. See the sidebar entitled "Understanding Slope Gradients" (page 35) for a refresher on how to do this.

☐ Plan a day that you can hike that trail. It is always safer and more fun when someone can go with you. You can share your newfound skills along the way.

- ☐ Tell someone you can trust that you are going hiking that day. Leave the following fundamental information with them (note that this is covered later in the book in great detail):
    - ☐ Where you are going.
    - ☐ When you expect to return.
    - ☐ Who you are going with.
    - ☐ Your phone number and the numbers of anyone in your group hiking with you.
    - ☐ The phone number of authorities responsible for a search if you get lost. Typically, this is a search-and-rescue team. If you are unsure, call the nonemergency number for local law enforcement of the area you are going to. They will let you know what entity is responsible for that area.

- ☐ Gather a fundamental survival and first aid kit. Note that this is also covered in great detail later in this book.

- ☐ Check the weather to see what you can expect on the day you wish to hike. Get appropriate clothing to handle whatever weather conditions are forecast.

- ☐ Before traveling to the area you wish to hike, hydrate yourself. How much water is needed is a highly debatable topic. However, a good rule of thumb for the average person is to have ½ gallon (1.9 L) of water per day on a normal day. You must add to this if you are expending lots of energy on a wilderness navigation trip.

- ☐ Travel to the site that you wish to hike. If it is public-access, you may need to pay a fee and/or register. This is for your safety. Do it.

- ☐ Find your parking spot on the map that you brought with you. Mark your parking location on the map.

- ☐ Orient your map to north by using a compass or other navigational aid. Note that many more aids will be detailed later in the book.

- ☐ Start at point A and begin your hike. Keep your map in a location in which you can easily access it.

- ☐ At every notable feature (such as a change in slope, a creek or a trail intersection), find it on your topography map. At each of these points, take a look at the contour lines and see how that applies to what is in front of you on the earth. Do a 360-degree check of these at each place you stop.

- [ ] Travel to point B. Note the features and topography that surround you.

- [ ] Stop at the ending point (when it is safe to do so) and take some notes about your experience. Enjoy being outdoors.

- [ ] You probably don't want to stay there forever, so let's get you back. Turn around and face the direction you want to travel back on.

- [ ] You will now need to orient your map to north again. The way you held the map on the way from point A to point B will be exactly opposite of the way you hold it going from point B to point A. For example, if you were holding the map and north farthest away from you, on the way back north will be closest to you. This is because north is north—for wilderness navigation needs, it does not change. Therefore, if you were traveling to the north on the way out, you will be traveling away from north on the way back.

BONUS

Reread the story at the beginning of this chapter. Consider how you could use skills from this chapter to keep yourself from experiencing similar tragedy. There are many things we will cover throughout this book, but here are a few from this chapter alone that can help you:

1. When leaving the trail, review the map and know where you are on it.

2. Note the general direction you are heading by utilizing the map. Along the way make some scuff marks on the ground.

3. At your stopping point, note where you are on the map.

4. Do whatever you came to that spot to do (use the bathroom, set up a tent, get a view of the area).

5. Before heading back, determine the direction you need to return. It will be 180 degrees from the direction you came in on. Walk that direction back to the spot where you left the trail. You could use pace count (covered in chapter 4) to determine how far you went in and how far you should come back out of the area.

CHAPTER 2

CHOOSING THE RIGHT COMPASS AND LEARNING HOW IT WORKS

Live your life by a compass, not a clock. —Anonymous

Tracy and I are quite fond of challenging each other in various ways to enhance our individual backcountry skill sets. He has a comfortable skill set when it comes to land navigation. This comfortability is not born out of some sort of luck but rather is one of determined focus, training and study. Many years ago, we discussed filming a segment for the Nature Reliance School YouTube channel to help people find their way out of situations in which they found themselves lost, which we called the "Lost Man Exercise." In this exercise, I blindfolded Tracy and drove him a few miles away to a location unknown to him. I then escorted him (still blindfolded) down an incredibly steep hill into an area that he was not familiar with. It was away from all known roads, trails and any other man-made imprint on the earth. Once we were there, he took the blindfold off, I handed him a 1:24000 USGS map. This map displayed several square miles of land in the heart of the Daniel Boone National Forest. The Daniel Boone National Forest sprawls over 708,000 acres (2,865 sq. km) of land, so it is easy to see that Tracy was virtually a needle in a haystack if someone were to try to find him. That, however, was not the point of the exercise. Our purpose was for Tracy to work through the process of finding himself in the most literal sense possible. His compass, along with the map I gave him, was an integral tool in accomplishing this task.

By filming this exercise, we obviously wanted others to learn from it, but it also had the bonus of putting Tracy under simulated stress. Being under stress can be a game changer when it comes to proper decision making. Tracy conquered it like a champ. At this point, his lost-proofing was a game of numbers more than anything. (Lost-proofing is the practice of systematically taking steps to ensure you do not get or stay lost. Rather than fall victim to the emotion of being lost, you will physically or mentally list the necessary steps to self-rescue. Then you'll go through the list to fix any issues.) I had taken Tracy into a very deep valley with a thick tree canopy on purpose: This did not allow him to find recognizable, tall land features easily.

First, Tracy took a compass directional heading down the long valley we were in. He then looked at the map and found a select few valleys on the map that had areas that corresponded to the directional headings he found and determined with his compass. We then began to walk one direction down this very long valley and, every time we came to another valley feeding into it, he would take a reading and match it up to his map. In this manner, he systematically broke down the map into usable portions. Using this process, Tracy took no more than thirty minutes to find his near-exact position on the map. It was quite an accomplishment, really, considering the stress that comes from walking through an unknown forest blindfolded. Did I mention that I stepped on a copperhead by accident on the way in? This also added to the excitement of the moment.

In this chapter, we want to help you learn about compasses. We will then start to combine our newfound knowledge from chapter 1 with the information in this one so that you can lost-proof yourself much like Tracy did.

After reading chapter 1, I am sure you can see that navigating in a wilderness with only a map is an efficient way of meeting your goals in outdoor travel. All that is required for most wilderness navigation is that you are aware of your surroundings and that you make frequent, regular checks on the map for your position. What happens if you are in the dark, in white-out snow conditions, in a desert, in a thick forest or under a jungle canopy? It will be nearly impossible to see the terrain features to adequately associate yourself with it. These are some of the reasons you should carry a compass. I think of it as quality assurance: The more tools I have to navigate with, the more quality navigation I am likely to have.

We have taught backcountry and wilderness-related skills to thousands of people and have noticed that people fall into one of four categories when it comes to the use of compasses. I have them listed in order, from most to least common:

- Those who have no idea how to use a compass; those who don't carry one and instead rely on their sense of direction or cell phone; those who never leave a marked trail or some combination of the three.

- Those who know that a compass is an important tool and carry it with them but who do not have the knowledge to use it.

- Those who have a compass but use it only sparingly. This group includes those who have had previous training (such as in the military) but have not kept up with the skills and are therefore not comfortable with them.

- Those who have received training or have taught themselves to use a compass and can navigate efficiently, safely and accurately. This group regularly practices with map and compass even when it is not needed to ensure they keep their skill set current.

The book you now hold, and this chapter, is a way to assist each of these groups of people in finding their way. Most who travel distances greater than a mile or so into a wilderness *know* that a compass is an important tool but simply do not know how to use it. This is because somewhere along the line, many have been told that a compass is a confusing and hard-to-learn piece of equipment. It is neither of those. We want to break compasses down into their simplest parts and then build them back up by the end of this chapter to remove some of the mystique surrounding compasses.

We learn in elementary school science class that the earth has North and South Poles. Many visualize this as the earth having flagpoles on its opposite ends. This is not the most accurate way of considering it. A better visualization is an incredibly long rod that extends through the entire earth. One end of that rod comes to the surface at the North Pole and the other end comes to the surface at the South Pole. There is a magnetic field that flows in the same general direction as the direction of the rod. That flow can be sensed by pieces of magnetized metal. That is why a magnetized piece of metal will be north-seeking (see image 18). The added confusion arises in

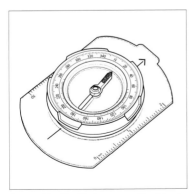

Image 18: Familiarize yourself with the north-seeking arrow on any compass you use.

Image 19: The North Pole movement over time.

when we realize that it does not point to the actual North Pole. Due to the ever-shifting magma within the earth's crust, the *magnetic* North Pole is always on the move. In image 19, you can see this difference. For navigation purposes, it is imperative that we understand that our compasses point toward magnetic north, and our maps are based on true and grid north.

There are two basic types of compasses, and both are useful tools in wilderness navigation. Lensatic compasses are those associated with military or similar tactical use, and baseplate compasses are the type most used by wilderness adventurers. In the following images, we will look at the pieces and parts of each. We will go over how to use these later in the chapter.

BASEPLATE COMPASSES

Baseplate compasses are the most common compasses used by nonmilitary wilderness navigators (see image 20). They have a clear plastic base in which all other parts of the compass are mounted. Brands vary greatly for baseplate compasses, but nearly all of them will have rulers that correspond to grid systems and or scales on maps. That is why you are likely to see

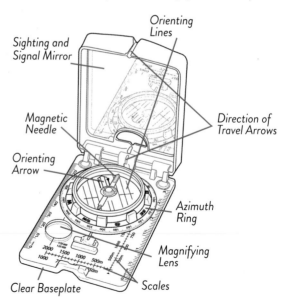

Orienting Lines

Sighting and Signal Mirror

Direction of Travel Arrows

Magnetic Needle

Orienting Arrow

Azimuth Ring

Magnifying Lens

Clear Baseplate

Scales

Image 20: Typical baseplate compass with sighting mirror.

HOW MUCH ACCURACY DO YOU NEED IN A COMPASS? WHAT IS "AIMING OFF"?

Engineers, surveyors and some foresters will need a high degree of accuracy for the work they do in the backcountry. Although 2 degrees on a typical baseplate compass is an acceptable level of accuracy for the average backcountry navigator, it does not work well enough to meet the uses of the other groups.

For example, let's assume you are given a compass heading and you travel on that heading for exactly 1 mile (1.6 km). If you travel in error 1 degree off in either direction, you will be 92 feet (28 m) from your destination when you get there. Considering the entire scope of things, 92 feet (28 m) is still within easy visual contact unless the areas is densely covered in undergrowth.

Therefore, "aiming off" is a very important principle to understand. Drifting off the intended direction of travel is an issue that even seasoned wilderness navigators will experience on a regular basis. Most wilderness navigators will purposely aim off left or right from their given destination when they are traveling away from a developed trail. This is not done haphazardly, though. Looking at a map, a navigator can find a feature such as a valley, river or ridgeline that will make it clear where they are when they come to it. They can then use that obvious feature to navigate, using terrain association (see page 33) and their compass, to the desired location. Many times, this new direction of travel will offer a safer or easier travel corridor.

1:24000 on the baseplate. That shows the scale on the baseplate will match exactly with a 1:24000 scale grid map. These compasses may also have a simple ruler on them. These serve to measure distances on the map for good quality control in your map reading.

BEZEL

The bezel is the dial that sits on top of the baseplate and rotates. This ring surrounds a housing that contains fluid, which allows the north-seeking needle to float freely. It is typically marked in 2-degree increments up to 360 degrees. Please note that 360 degrees is most often marked with an N, which represents north on the bezel. This does not mean that wherever you find the N, it is pointing toward magnetic north. That is what the needle is for.

The typical baseplate compass does not have much room to show all the different measurement options on it. It would be too many numbers on a small piece of equipment. The numbers would all run together. Therefore, the tick marks reference increments of 2 degrees. Also, the four cardinal measurements are not actually listed and are replaced by an alpha character designation:

- North = 0 degrees or 360 degrees, since it is the beginning and the end of the measurements.

- East = 90 degrees.

- South = 180 degrees.

- West = 270 degrees.

DIRECTION-OF-TRAVEL ARROW

When holding a compass in your hand, you should hold it in such a way that the direction of travel is pointing away from your body. As its name implies, this is the direction in which you want to travel.

NORTH-SEEKING NEEDLE

Inside the housing is a magnetized needle that is north-seeking. This allows a user to have a point of reference, no matter where they are on the planet. On most models of baseplate compasses, this needle will be slender and red. If you own or look at other brands, the needle can be many different colors and can come in different shapes. Pay special attention when the compass is held level and you rotate your body. The north-seeking needle should continue to point in the same direction.

ORIENTING ARROW AND LINES

Within the bezel housing, you will see the orienting arrow and lines parallel to it. This will be used to orient your map and compass together appropriately. By orienting the two together, you will be able to transfer information from map to compass and compass to map accurately. We will cover in detail how to do so in this and later chapters.

SIGHTING MIRROR OR WIRE

A simple baseplate compass will cover most of your on-trail needs. Remember, the compass is primarily a tool to help us have better terrain association and quality use of our map. When we do need to go off-trail, having a compass that has a sighting mirror (or wire in the lensatic compass) will help us be more accurate when taking our readings. Compasses that have a sighting mirror are commonly referred to as prismatic compasses. The sighting mirror will have three distinct parts to it:

- The mirror is inside the hinged piece that covers the bezel. Mirrors allow for a user to be much more accurate. You hold the compass (see image 21), fold the mirror so you can still view the north and orienting arrows and sight in the point in which you want to travel.

- The "gunsight" allows you to more accurately get a sight picture of that same point. The gunsight portion will be in the shape of a V, which gives you a quick visual reference. You can then sight a distant object (e.g., a valley, mountaintop and so on) very directly.

Image 21: Each person will find the appropriate distance from their eye and still see the compass reading clearly.

- The sighting line is another piece of your prismatic compass that is used to help gain more accuracy. While sighting your compass, it helps to bring your eye from the compass reading up to the gunsight. It also serves as a visual reminder to keep your compass level rather than leaning one direction or the other.

53

BASEPLATE COMPASS: WHO IS RED FRED AND WHY IS HE IN A SHED?

An *azimuth* is the horizontal angle or direction of a compass. It is the reading you will set on your compass to navigate from one point of direction or interest to another. You do this differently for each of the different types of compasses (baseplate versus lensatic). Many wilderness navigation instructors will help their students remember how to use a baseplate specifically by using a mnemonic to help them remember how to do it. It is called "Red Fred in the Shed."

As a means of quality control, ensure that the measurement you are about to transfer to your compass is a magnetic measurement, not a grid/map measurement. For ease of learning, we will show on the associated images here an azimuth reading of 100 degrees magnetic.

1. Baseplate (see image 22): Once you get your magnetic azimuth, turn the dial on your compass until that number is directly under the index line associated with the direction of travel. "Red Fred" is the north-seeking arrow on your baseplate compass. Since most compasses utilize a red arrow to signify this, the north arrow is commonly referred to as Red Fred. The "shed" is the orienting arrow inside of the bezel housing. It is tall and has a point on it near the ring. With a little imagination, you can see that it resembles a tall shed. Now that you have the compass properly set to the right azimuth, hold your compass properly and turn your body until Red Fred is in the shed. The direction

Image 22: Baseplate compass set to 100°.

Image 23: Lensatic compass set to 100°.

that your direction-of-travel arrow is pointing is the azimuth you should navigate along.

2. **Lensatic (see image 23):** Since a lensatic compass does not have these same pieces, setting and using an azimuth is a different process. Rotate the compass until the azimuth you need falls directly under the black line that is fixed on your glass cover. Turn the bezel ring until the luminous line is directly in line with your north-seeking arrow.

CLINOMETER ARROW

If you look inside the bezel of your baseplate compass, you will see another arrow (typically, it is black), which is referred to as the clinometer arrow. This arrow is utilized to determine the angle of a slope on a geographic element on the earth. This is a common practice for surveying crews to get an approximation of distance along a slope. Imagine you are looking at a topography map that contains several elevation changes. Going from one point on the map to another does not take into consideration the slope or angle of the hill or mountainside. By understanding the angle of that slope, you can then determine more accurately the distance along that slope. It also tells you the angle you will be traveling should you need to travel directly up or down a slope.

SCALES

Along the sides and base of baseplate compasses, you will find scales. These scales relate directly to scales of maps. You can, therefore, use your compass to be the measuring device for determining distances on the map.

Baseplate compasses were originally designed and manufactured to be utilized as orienteering compasses. Orienteering itself is a learning methodology for both beginner and advanced wilderness navigation. Orienteering compasses are lightweight and useful for that sort of application. Lensatic compasses have been around for a lot longer. They have been used extensively by the military and tactical-user groups that employ them in basic training and beyond in military careers. Those are many of the same users that have taught others how to do land navigation throughout the world (and the United States in particular). Because of the lensatic compass's popularity, understanding it may be the way you want to go as well.

MAKING YOUR OWN COMPASS NEEDLE

The same magnetism that attracts a compass needle will attract any magnetized needle, including one that you make yourself. Here are the simple steps to do so (see image 24):

1. Gather a sewing needle, magnet, water, a non-magnetic container and a thin item that floats, such as a leaf or thin piece of bark. The stronger the magnet, the better.

2. Stroke the length of the needle with the magnet. Ensure that you only stroke it in only one direction. This will magnetize the needle.

3. Put the water in the container and place the thin item that floats on it. You could also use a piece of paper, but be aware it will quickly absorb water and sink. The item in the water should have enough room to float freely.

4. Place the magnetized needle in the container on the floating item. The magnetized needle will be drawn to point toward magnetic north.

Image 24: You can magnetize a needle and float it to get an approximate north-south line.

VARIOUS TERMS FOR COMPASS READINGS

Some of the following terms are used interchangeably. That should not be the case. You should know the slight differences in these terms, as they are important. This is especially true when you are working with or communicating information to others. Please keep in mind that there are slight variations in these terms; however, the majority who do wilderness navigation will use the following terms interchangeably:

1. *Azimuth*: This is the horizontal angle or direction of what you are reading on the compass. The amount will be a number between 0 degrees and 360 degrees. This is the most accurate word that should be employed when using a compass. If you are given a measurement (e.g., 275 degrees) to be used on your compass, this means your azimuth is 275 degrees and you should set your compass accordingly and then use it to navigate.

2. *Heading*: This term is typically used in relation to something that is moving. It is the direction your nose is pointing while traveling. This is the nose on your face, canoe, drone or vehicle.

3. *Bearing*: This is a measurement usually stated as it relates to one of the four primary cardinal directions. For instance, a 45-degree azimuth would be known as northeast. Some go so far as to relate a bearing to one of the four cardinal directions. Our 45-degree azimuth could also be 45 degrees north, meaning that the measurement in question is 45 degrees from north.

LENSATIC COMPASSES

Lensatic compasses are very often referred to as military compasses (see image 25). Cammenga is the patent owner and manufacturer of top-quality lensatic compasses; nearly all others that we have seen are poor imitations. Although both lensatic and baseplate compasses are designed to guide direction, they are used in entirely different ways. Many lensatic compasses are carried by military users or those with that type of background or interest. They are heavy in comparison to other compasses and for good reason. They need to be able to withstand the incredible amount of abuse that warfare might bring to them. Cammenga's lensatic compasses were the first to offer tritium-illuminated needles, so they are easy to see at night without first being energized by a light source. The downside to this is that tritium is a radioactive material and has a half-life of approximately twelve years. If a compass contains 100 millicuries of tritium, in twelve years it will only contain 50 millicuries and so on until it has no illumination to it at all.

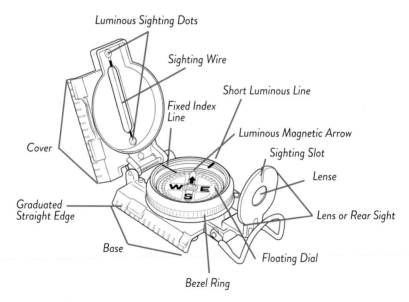

Image 25: Typical lensatic compass.

The important parts of a lensatic compass are detailed in the following sections.

THUMB LOOP

The thumb loop serves two important functions. The first is to secure the compass when it is in the closed position. The second is to place your thumb inside of the loop when you are holding the compass in position to sight objects or take an azimuth.

COVER

When the cover is closed it serves to protect the face of the compass and it locks the needle in place. It also contains the sighting wire.

SIGHTING WIRE

The sighting wire is what sets a lensatic compass apart from other options available. The sighting wire allows the user to sight in objects for determining or utilizing a known azimuth. The wire is taut and able to withstand fair amounts of abuse. It provides the user the ability to obtain very accurate readings.

BEZEL RING

The bezel ring is the ring on top that holds the glass cover. It also contains two lines that allow the user to preset a direction for nighttime navigation. By turning the bezel, you will note that it has a "click" that is both audible and tactile. There are 120 clicks, each one representing 3 degrees of change.

BLACK INDEX LINE

The black index line is a stationary line that helps in determining direction. When the compass is held correctly, the azimuth that is found directly under the black index line identifies the direction the compass is pointing.

COMPASS DIAL

The compass dial is the free-floating piece within the compass housing that contains the measurements on it. The red scales measure degrees; the black scales are milliradians and are typically used for tactically inclined individuals (such as artillery personnel and machine gunners).

FIXING COMMON PROBLEMS WHEN HOLDING A BASEPLATE COMPASS

You can have the greatest compass in the world, but if you do not hold it properly, it will not work the way it was intended. By following these simple steps, you can hold it properly and avoid many of the common pitfalls:

1. Pay special attention to anything metallic or magnetic that is close to your compass when you're using it. Some common problems are watches, neck knives, metallic bracelets and even being too close to your vehicle when using the compass.

2. When holding your compass, ensure that the magnetic needle floats freely. If you rotate your body, the needle should continue to point north.

3. If you have a baseplate without a sighting mirror, you can utilize the center-hold method for stabilizing it. This means you hold it near your sternum and look down on the bezel to see your reading.

4. Do not turn the direction-of-travel arrow away from you at an angle. This is one of the most common mistakes that I see our students making. We are quick to gently remind them of the correct way. Put the compass in your hand and at your sternum and utilize the compass much like a turret that is turning. The compass should generally not point in a direction other than the one in which you are facing. It is difficult to get an accurate direction-of-travel heading by looking at your compass from the side.

USING COMPASSES AND MAPS OUTSIDE NORTH AMERICA

There are a few things you should know about wilderness navigation outside North America:

1. Declination is an effect all over the world—magnetism is affected east or west based on your location. Know what your declination is before transferring readings from map to compass or the reverse.

2. Compass dip, also called inclination, is the effect in which your compass needle dips on one side or the other. If you go far north or south, your needle will literally dip so much that it will no longer float freely. There are actually "balancing zones" throughout the world that compasses are best suited for. Most compass technology today compensates for this effect. For example, my preferred manufacturer (Suunto) has two zone compasses: one for the Northern Hemisphere, one for the Southern Hemisphere. Suunto also makes a third one that is weighted in such a way that it can be used throughout the world. This type of compass is typically referred to as a global compass. If the place you are purchasing from does not list the zone you will be using the compass in, you can request that information.

3. Maps are not freely available in other places of the world. When they are, they rarely have the detail we are accustomed to on USGS topographic maps. Scaling is also different. In North America, particularly in the United States, our maps are readily available in 1:24000 detail. This is rare in other countries.

4. We have used the metric system and Imperial measuring system throughout this book. In other countries, all measurements will be metric.

METHODS TO PUT YOUR MAP AND COMPASS TO WORK

All wilderness navigators need to regularly practice some basic navigation techniques. There are certain types of people that regularly come to our wilderness navigation classes. Most of our students are brand-new to land navigation. They have a compass and maybe a trail map, but they don't have a solid and usable skill set. We also get a number of people who "used" to have skill in these techniques and methods, but they have lost them. Wilderness navigation is definitely a perishable skill set. The exercises in chapters 9, 10 and 11 will help you either learn or brush up on your skills. For now, note that there are three primary methods of wilderness navigation. Taken or used together as a whole, they will allow you as a wilderness navigator to make your way into and out of a wilderness safely. The three primary methods of wilderness navigation are as follows:

- **Terrain association:** As discussed in the previous chapter, terrain association is a process by which a wilderness navigator uses the terrain features on a map and associates them with the geography that is in front of him or her. This is a very quick method to know your location.

- **Dead reckoning:** This is the process of being given—or determining in the field—an azimuth, then following that azimuth until you arrive at the destination. This does not take into consideration anything in the terrain as being a barrier or otherwise problematic to navigate through. The steps for dead reckoning are simple to follow and easy to do solo or with a partner:

  - Determine what your starting and ending points are on your map.

  - Determine your grid azimuth going from your starting point to your ending point. Since you will be using your compass, be sure to adjust for declination.

  - Use the scale on your map and determine the distance from your starting location to your destination. For ease of counting, convert your measurement into steps in your pace count.

  - Set the needed azimuth on the compass (see the sidebar on page 54).

  - Pick something in front of you that lies directly on the azimuth you are reading.

- Keep track of your pace count as you walk to the object. Once there, take another reading but continue your pace count.

- If you stay on that azimuth, you will arrive at your destination once you have reached the appropriate number of steps.

- **Combination:** This method is by far the best way to navigate. With it, you will essentially do dead reckoning. The primary difference is that anytime you have a prominent feature on the geography, you identify this object on the map along with your navigation route. Terrain association and dead reckoning are both quality methods on their own. When you put them together, you increase your accuracy and quality control.

Some other basic navigation techniques will prove useful. Consider the following techniques:

- **Leapfrogging** is the practice of taking an azimuth and utilizing a partner to keep you online with it. To do this, partner A sets their compass and places themselves on the line facing the direction they want to travel. Partner B goes out close to the line as far as they can go and still have good communication with partner A. This communication can be done via voice, radio or hand signals. Partner B then turns and faces partner A. Partner A then communicates with partner B on how to get on the line. Once partner B is on the line, partner A will tell them to hold and move up beyond that position and the roles are reversed. In this manner, the two partners can very efficiently keep their azimuth and move along it without stopping.

- **Determine a destination.** Once you know what your destination is, you should verify it on the map and on the ground in front of you whenever possible. Coupled with good situational awareness, this is a primary method for maintaining good-quality navigation. If for some reason you lose sight of your objective destination, you will need to account for that. You will then adjust yourself to get back on the azimuth that was intended.

- **Logging along the azimuth.** If you take time to log prominent features along with your route, you will have quality-control points along the way, not just at the finish. Since most wilderness navigation is done in an environment where you cannot see your objective destination, this practice is especially helpful.

DETERMINING DIRECTION WITH A CAN OF SOUP

This method is most often done by utilizing an analog watch. You don't need an analog watch, however—you can use a digital one or even a cell phone. All you need the watch for is to give you an accurate time. Here are the steps (note that this method applies to the Northern Hemisphere):

1. Determine the time with any device you have available to you.

2. Draw (or imagine) the hour hands on your can of soup so that they depict the current time at which you are determining this direction.

3. The imaginary hour hand should point to the sun.

4. Draw an imaginary line that is midway between the hour hand and the imaginary position of 12:00 on the soup can.

5. The imaginary line that is drawn will be pointing south.

Image 26: Knowing the time is 4:00 p.m., point the "hour hand" at the sun. The line that bisects 4:00 p.m., and the sun is south in the Northern Hemisphere.

Please note that in the Southern Hemisphere, you will need to point the 12:00 position toward the sun. The line that is the midway point between 12:00 and the hour hand will be pointing north.

- **Find a backstop or catching feature.** Whenever possible, determine a feature on your map slightly beyond your objective destination that is incredibly obvious. If you reach it, you will realize you have traveled past the destination and can adjust before going too far. An example of this is a river or road that is on your map beyond the point at which you want to stop. If you come upon the river or road, you have gone beyond your designated stopping point.

- **Handrailing is a similar methodology.** This involves utilizing a feature on the ground (such as a waterway, cliff line or ridge) that you can parallel. Your distance from the handrail will vary as the terrain varies. This gives you a quick reference point to ensure your quality of travel.

This chapter has been a detailed look at the physical components of compasses. These first three chapters are much like the assembly instructions you get for household items—often disregarded until needed. Do not do that with these chapters. You will save time, frustration and possibly your life if you develop a good understanding of these tools first. You can be assured that we will teach you the skills to utilize them effectively as we move along.

TROUBLESHOOTING: OVERCOMING COMMON PROBLEMS WITH COMPASSES

We have been teaching land navigation at our school for several years now, which has given us opportunity to see that a large number of wilderness navigation problems arise out of the misuse of a compass. There are several things that go wrong; thankfully, these issues also have easy answers. If you are new to utilizing a compass, you should double-check everything you do with it. It is a simple thing to do, but it works. If you set your compass for a heading, stop what you are doing before you use it and go through the process again. It is a worthwhile investment of time to double-check. Once you get more comfortable utilizing the compass, you will know when it is time for you to stop doing everything twice. When time and situations allow, we double-check our settings and measurements before utilizing them. That is a general protocol that will prevent a lot of issues for you. Following are some additional problems you may face when using your compass.

NOT HOLDING THE COMPASS PROPERLY

The way you hold your compass affects its accuracy and usefulness. Use the following tips to ensure you're holding your compass properly (if you'd like more tips specific to baseplate compasses, see the sidebar on page 54):

- When holding your compass, ensure that the magnetic north-seeking needle floats freely. If you rotate your body, the needle should continue to point north.

- The center-hold method is a fairly good way to hold a compass. However, a cheek hold is better and more accurate. Center-hold means you hold the compass near your sternum and look down on the bezel to see your reading. Cheek hold

Image 27: Sighting your direction of travel from the side opens the user to inaccuracies. Do not use it this way.

means you hold it up in front of your face and sight directly from one eye. (How far to hold the compass from your face will be determined by your eyesight more than anything.)

- Do not turn the direction-of-travel arrow away from you at an angle (image 27). This is one of the most common mistakes that new navigators make. Put the compass in your hand and at your sternum and utilize the compass much like a turret that is turning. The compass should not point in a direction other than the one in which you are facing. It is nearly impossible to get an accurate direction-of-travel heading by looking at your compass from the side.

FUN AND NOT-SO-FUN ISSUES WITH MAGNETISM

The needle on your compass is magnetized—this we all know. But what we may not all know is that that magnetism can be the root of a host of issues. Do not have metallic and other magnetized items next to your compass. Here are some helpful tips that are often overlooked:

- Do not wear rings on your fingers. This proves to be an issue most often when you center-hold your compass. If you lay the compass in the palm of your hand and you have a metallic ring on, it could pull the needle slightly off.

- Watch your watch. Watches will also pull the needle off, especially watches that also give direction.

- Be aware of what is around your neck. Neck knives and other attachments to necklaces will prove to be problematic if your compass is held close to them.

- If your family, unit or team stores multiple compasses (even training ones) lying on top of one another, they will most likely "spring" and not be accurate. We store our compasses in a container that has a foam liner so that all the compasses are held in place and they do not stay in contact with one another (image 28).

- When utilizing a compass on a table, make sure your compass is not over or close to metallic table components (such as braces, bolts and so on). You can slide your compass along the table and see it change direction when it is over these metallic parts.

- If you use a clipboard in the field, ensure you take measurements with your compass away from the retaining clip. We prefer to not use clipboards at all for this very reason. Some navigators will do this as a learning tool when they first start, however.

- Do not take readings in proximity to large metallic objects. This could include cars, metal buildings and flagpoles or light poles.

- Be careful when taking readings under electric power lines. This does not always affect the readings, but we have noticed interference under high-volume transmission lines.

Image 28: If you have a number of compasses, do not store them against one another.

The preceding are some items and scenarios that affect the actual compass itself. We need to also consider the common problems that arise when using a compass. By looking at the typical baseplate compass, you will note that most of them have a red north-seeking arrow. Some are black, white, yellow or another color. When you purchase your compass, you need to make sure to verify your compass's accuracy and confirm which is the north-seeking arrow. Although this seems obvious, when you are out navigating in a wilderness this can easily cause issues. Here are some reasons why:

- The colors on the north-seeking arrow can fade over time. If you do not look at your compass regularly, you may not realize which side is which. Many compasses will utilize red on the north-seeking arrow and black or white on the south arrow. When the colors fade, the arrows may be more golden in color. You can either get another compass or just recognize that is the case and ensure you know for certain which arrow is north-seeking. We feel it's best to carry a compass whose components and colors are as close to mint as possible—if you ever experience the high degree of stress that comes with being lost in the wilderness, you will need to be able to quickly and easily locate and use the north-seeking arrow.

- Even if the arrows are of the right color, when you get tired it is easy to mistakenly align the south end of the north-seeking arrow with the orienting arrow. When you have been out hiking or working in a wilderness setting and you set your compass for azimuth, make sure you use the north-seeking arrow. It is easy to put the south arrow in the "red shed." That is why the "Red Fred in the shed" phrase can prove helpful. Set the azimuth on your compass, then put it down. Confirm your measurement from the source you got it from (e.g., map, GPS, notes, radio), then look at your compass again to ensure the setting is correct.

- Your declination amount can easily put you several degrees off course if you fail to account for it. One way to assist you with this is to refer to your readings as map north, magnetic north or grid north.

- It is also very easy to correct for declination in the wrong direction. As an example, in my location our rounded declination is 6 degrees west. This means that when I get a reading from my map, I add 6 degrees to it. If I were to adjust for declination in the wrong direction, I would be 12 degrees off my magnetic reading needed. Let's assume that I have a map reading of 150 degrees. Adjusting for declination would give me 156 degrees on my compass. If, however, I adjust the wrong direction, I would have 144 degrees on my compass. That is the full 12 degrees off from what I should be utilizing on my compass.

QUESTIONS FOR PRACTICE

1. "Red Fred in the Shed" is a mnemonic that helps us to do what?

2. The north needle on a compass will always point in which direction?

3. The V notch on some compasses is used for what?

4. What degree on a compass represents due south?

5. Ninety degrees represent which direction on a compass?

6. Why is it important to hold your compass level?

7. The thin wire on a lensatic compass is used for what?

8. Each tick mark on a baseplate compass represents how many degrees?

9. True or false: Many compasses will develop bubbles in the housing but this poses no problems for its accuracy.

10. Name at least one thing not mentioned in this text that will pull a compass off?

Answers: (1) It reminds us to put the north-seeking arrow (Red Fred) inside the orienting arrow (shed) to set our compass's azimuth for traveling. **(2)** Magnetic north. **(3)** Sighting. **(4)** 180 degrees. **(5)** Due east. **(6)** So the compass arrow floats freely. **(7)** Sighting. **(8)** 2 degrees. **(9)** False. The bubble within the housing will always affect the accuracy of your compass readings. **(10)** All-terrain vehicles, powerlines, metallic pieces used to fuse broken bones.

GET OUT AND PRACTICE

The following is a step-by-step process for you to begin developing wilderness navigation skills by utilizing a map and compass outside. The first steps are the same as the preceding chapter. Here are the highlights if you don't remember.

☐ Find a familiar or new location to practice. It will be best if there are some open areas.

☐ Get a good map and verify datum, grid and other pertinent information you learned in the preceding chapter.

☐ Take a friend if you like, but definitely tell a friend the important information. At the very least this should include where you are going, when you expect to return and whom you are going with.

☐ Take the necessary gear for safety, survival and any weather conditions that the forecast predicts.

☐ Go to a central spot that allows you to travel out in various directions.

☐ Randomly choose four directions. Choose directions in which you can generally travel northeast, southeast, southwest and then northwest. Choose a random distance for each direction.

☐ Use your map and a pencil to mark where your starting point is and these four directions. (If you have a laminated or taped map, you can do this with a dry-erase marker.) Draw these four lines on your map and use your scale to measure the random distance you determined for each.

☐ In a notebook, create a log of which features you should recognize along each azimuth (e.g., traveling uphill, traveling downhill, crossing a creek and so on).

☐ Travel each of the azimuths, and verify your location with your log. At each notable feature, stop, look at the terrain and note your pace count.

☐ To navigate back to the central point, you will use a back azimuth. It is exactly 180 degrees difference from the original random degrees you determined. At the end of each short hike, set your compass for the back azimuth and use the same techniques to navigate back to the central point.

☐ Follow each of the azimuths and use your pace count. Utilize terrain association to the best of your ability and see if your pace count is accurate in different terrains.

☐ Once afield, find a notable man-made or natural feature that also appears on your map. This could be a hill, cell tower or building. At random intervals during your hikes, stop and take a magnetic reading from your position to that feature. Remember this is a magnetic reading. Now calculate your declination variation and place your line on your map from the notable feature.

These are some of the ways you can start putting your map and compass to work in tandem. In the next chapter, we will be adding a GPS unit to the mix. At the end of that chapter, you will see that there are more ways you can practice using your map, compass and add GPS—but remember, you don't have to employ GPS. A map with grid lines and your compass are the two tools that make land navigation much easier. The GPS that we will add next offers more quality assurance to the process, though, which is a good thing.

CHAPTER 3

UNDERSTANDING GLOBAL POSITIONING SYSTEMS AND OTHER USEFUL TECHNOLOGICAL EQUIPMENT

Intuition is the GPS of life. —Donald L. Hicks

In 2016, a Pennsylvania family traveled to Bryce Canyon National Park in Utah for vacation. During their travels in the park, they came to a forest road that was closed. Their GPS offered another road as an alternative, which they decided to take. The alternative turned out to be snow covered and eventually proved to be impassable. Not very far from the turnoff, they became stuck and unable to drive farther.

The family determined they would hike their way out to safety. It was a daunting 26-mile (42-km) journey, during which the family stayed alive by sheer will, a small amount of outdoor training and, no doubt, a fair bit of luck.

When they were later interviewed by the sheriff about the incident, he was quick to point out that it happens all the time in that area. The sheriff accurately noted that GPS devices do not register all roads that are closed.

GPSs are exactly that, a system or network of components that provide a user with the tools they need to know where they are anywhere on the planet. GPSs are tools and have no cognitive capability. That is why you should use as much intuition as you can along with the tool to get you safely to your destination.

Let's break down GPS tools to understand them a little better. There are three components that make up the GPS system:

- **Satellites:** Information currently available to the public states there is a total of twenty-four GPS satellites that orbit approximately 13,000 miles (20,900 km) above the surface of the earth. These satellites are in specific orbital patterns such that at any one time, you should be able to contact at least five of those satellites with a receiver (these satellites continually emit a signal). The satellites are placed there by government agencies and were originally intended for government use. It is assumed that there are more satellites designated for the sole use of the US Department of Defense.

- **Controllers:** The US Air Force is responsible for controlling these satellites and their orbits. The controllers are found in five separate locations around the world. The controllers also ensure that the satellites are transmitting properly.

- **Handheld units:** This is the portion of the system that we think of as a GPS, although, as you can see, it involves all three of these integral parts. Handheld units typically receive information from the satellites and put it into usable information on the unit. The latest available technology allows some units to be able to transmit small bits of text information as well. These types of units typically have a subscription service to go along with the cost of the unit itself.

There are four main types of GPS units in common use by civilians today. I have ranked these in order of reliability, with the most dependable being first (as noted later, as cell phone apps become more advanced, they will most likely surpass the others in all areas in the very near future):

- Non-mapping units are those that give you only data. They have no topography and little mapping capability. The data offered consists of coordinates, distances and directional bearings. These GPS systems are more commonly used with some sort of paper map and are the type I use most often. Mine is a Garmin Foretrex 401. I have worked with many military and law-enforcement units that use these Garmin products with success. It is worth noting that Tracy has a Garmin Foretrex 401 that has multiple issues. At this point, after seeing so many others that work well, I believe his particular unit to be an anomaly; however, it does highlight the need for you to regularly get out and use your device—even if it is just for practice. This will ensure your unit is functioning well when you need it.

- Mapping units are those that integrate topography maps into the handheld device. These come at a much higher cost, but they give the user the option to not carry a map. Even though this option is convenient, we lean on the side of safety and carry a paper topo map as a backup. Garmin makes a wide range of products that offer topography maps. One of my instructors also had a career in the special forces, and he utilized Garmin's line of eTrex GPSs throughout his time in the military. They take a fair amount of use and abuse and perform the positioning tasks very well. The topography maps that are offered on these units are precise but will take some getting used to if you are conditioned to a typical phone screen. Touch-screen GPS units are too expensive to be affordable for the average adventurer at this point. You will need to learn how to use a joystick for most GPS receivers. I have had one mapping-unit GPS, and I ended up donating it to a search-and-rescue team. I personally found it difficult to use the topography map on the unit itself. I regularly found myself only utilizing the data features on it. Therefore, I still stick with my non-mapping unit along with a paper map. Tracy and I have discussed the importance of carrying a paper map often, as he regularly goes on search-and-rescue events. Many searchers today are utilizing apps on their phones only. In his and my opinions, this is a problem waiting to happen.

- Multi-units are those that serve not only as a GPS but also as a compass, barometer, altimeter, radio or combination of any of those. As you would expect, these units pack a lot of technology into a single unit and are very costly for the typical user. The Garmin Rino units have been combining these needs into one receiver for many years now. I got one when they first came out. It worked well but ate battery like a champ. Those technological issues have been fixed in modern devices. Since you have so many tools (radio, GPS, compass, barometer, altimeter) all in one, if you happen to lose the unit, if it breaks down, or if you run out of batteries, you are left without multiple tools. I hope we have made it abundantly clear that a map and compass should always be included in your packing lists. I must admit that I am very mindful of safety. Therefore, I don't like putting all my eggs in one basket when it comes to a multi-unit. I prefer a smaller data unit, along with a map. That way, I have backup if one tool fails for some reason.

- Cell phone apps are applications that you download and use on your phone. As cell phones and other handheld computers become more technologically sound, they offer users the ability to use them as a GPS receiver as well. There are good paid and free apps available—see the sidebar on page 76 for more info.

TOP CELL PHONE APPS TO USE IN WILDERNESS NAVIGATION

At the time of this writing, GPS receivers and cell phone apps designed for that purpose are equally as accurate and useful. This requires your cell phone to be a GPS receiver. Some cell phones on the market today still use cell phone tower pings to triangulate your position and give you coordinates. Check with your retailer or the available specification charts online to verify that your cell phone has dedicated GPS technology. Please do not rely on these or any technological equipment as your sole navigation equipment.

Following are a few options with approximate prices if you'd like to download a GPS app to your phone:

1. Gaia GPS ($19.99/year): This is one GPS app that I like and prefer during backcountry use. It allows you to easily switch between topo, road and even national park maps. You can download as many maps as you like. This app also syncs with your Gaia online account, so you can preplan a trip and put the map on your device. You can also save points of travel while you are out adventuring and after you sync it, those same points will be available online as well.

2. Declination (free): This app will assist you in determining declination for any location on Earth. If you travel far distances on a regular basis, this app will prove incredibly useful in helping you know how to accurately adjust going from grid to magnetic or vice versa.

3. MapMyHike (free): This is a great app for the casual user who wants something to track their hikes for exercise. I use this app on my rucks and day hikes to keep up with distance traveled and calories burned. You can save routes and then compare your increase (or decrease) in efforts.

4. Spyglass ($3.99): This is an augmented-reality app that is useful for all outdoor excursions, including tactical exercises. It has the typical things you would expect on a good GPS app, such as maps, a gyrocompass and a waypoint tracker. It also has a tactical GPS layer, sniper range finder and coordinate converter.

5. Maplets ($3.00): This is a database collection of popular maps ranging from wilderness areas to streets.

6. **Trail Maps by National Geographic (pricing varies):** This is a reliable GPS-ready database covering the United States. It allows for the setting of waypoints, tracking and elevation profiles. At the time of this writing, you can access National Geographic's maps through either the Gaia GPS app or Avenza Maps app.

7. **Compass Pro ($1.00):** This is a compass substitute and allows some customization. It is important to understand that while the app has interesting and attractive features (such as Google Maps view), at the time of this writing, all compass apps can easily be wrong with the current technology available to civilians. In the near future, good apps will be available to all users.

8. **Google Maps or Apple Maps (free):** These mapping apps are the ones that come with your phone. They are best for road travel and possibly on-trail use. I would not suggest using them for regular hiking trips, as they do not provide the detail needed for accuracy. As an example, there is no easy way to access grid points for your location using these apps. They do allow the user to see where they are on a map, but if you were navigating to a location, they are not user-friendly for determining angles and such.

GPSs are one of the greatest *and* one of the worst things to happen to wilderness navigation. Our opening story illustrated how they can be one of the worst. They are one of the greatest because they offer trained users the ability to easily determine coordinates nearly anywhere on the planet. As we mentioned earlier, "death by GPS" is a growing problem. Many outdoor adventurers are taking the technology with them and only have a cursory understanding of how it works. This has led to many lost persons and fatalities in the wilderness. In this chapter, we are going to go over the common issues that must be overcome when relying on GPSs. We also want you to learn how to use them more effectively. This chapter is placed after chapters 1 and 2 for good reason: If you have skipped ahead to learn about GPS, you are making a common mistake. Go back and read those chapters before continuing. To understand the proper use of GPS devices, you must have a good understanding of mapping, grids and compass use. Here are some common problems people encounter when using GPSs:

• GPSs contain dozens of various datums and grid systems. If your GPS is on one of these systems and your map or the people you are communicating with are on another, you are talking different languages. If you don't understand what datums and grid systems are, please go back and read chapter 1 again.

- If your GPS does not contain maps, or you have difficulty interpreting them, then you will have much difficulty utilizing a GPS to navigate. A GPS unit does not interpret topography very well. If you follow it to a waypoint, it will point directly at that point and want you to follow that direction. It does not cognitively know that the route may be impassable. That direction may take you over a cliff, through a lake, or some other topography that cannot be traveled. You will need to know how to navigate around such obstacles.

- GPSs depend entirely on satellite technology to provide information for coordinates. If the satellites cannot be reached due to weather conditions, high cliffs, government shutdowns or similar hindrances, you will not have an effective tool.

- GPSs are electronic devices that run on batteries. This means that they are susceptible to running out of power or to becoming ineffective due to water infiltration of the units themselves.

- Cell phones that still require cell phone receptions for map use are susceptible to inaccuracies in the wilderness. If you are purchasing a phone and think you might want to use it for navigation, check with the seller to see if the GPS is actually a true GPS. A true GPS receives data from satellites and therefore does not require cell tower reception.

The preceding are situations that you need to be aware of if you are going to use a GPS. We are not going to leave you hanging, though. We are going to help you resolve each of those issues and many more. We specifically want to address these concerns before getting into the various options available with GPS units.

DATUMS AND GRID SYSTEMS

In chapter 1, we discussed the various datum sets and grid systems and their importance. When you get a GPS and use it for the first time, it will have a default setting for each. One of the first things you need to do is change the defaults to the datum and grid system you are most likely to use. If you are using a paper map, you should coordinate your GPS to whatever datum and grid system it uses.

THE BACKDOOR METHOD FOR CONVERTING ONE GRID SYSTEM TO ANOTHER

One issue that has come up when we have been working with various first responders (such as law-enforcement and search-and-rescue teams) is a lack of consistency on grid systems used across agencies. This sometimes occurs within the same agency as well when you have air assets communicating to ground assets. Inconsistency can be overcome by administration agreeing across-the-board on what should be utilized by all involved. Until that red-tape issue can be remedied, the following are simple steps you can take to convert any grid coordinate to another system:

1. Save a waypoint on your GPS and name it something that's easy to recall. The waypoint is then saved in the grid system that is currently set in that unit.

2. Now go into your unit settings and switch to the other grid system you need.

3. Pull up the saved waypoint from the first step. It will now read in the new units needed.

4. The preceding process does not change the waypoint position in any way. It only changes the grid system used to designate it. This can also be done for waypoints that are already saved in the unit to easily get a different coordinate system. It is even easier to do in most apps, as the coordinate system is usually a drop-down menu on most hiking and topo apps. Therefore, you can toggle between coordinate systems rather easily.

Some GPS receivers will have multiple screens (like my Garmin Foretrex 401), in which I can have a primary screen that relates the grid system I prefer to use and another screen that shows other grid systems. Since most aircraft pilots are Lat/Long users, I keep the secondary screen set to Lat/Long. With a couple clicks on the menu, I can go from one grid system to another without saving waypoints. Keep in mind this is true only for my current position at the time.

GPS SANS MAP

If your GPS does not offer mapping, or you are not carrying a separate map, you should fix that problem. In my opinion, a GPS used in concert with a good map is the preferred choice—you then have two ways to help you determine where you are in a wilderness. If one of them fails (e.g., the GPS batteries die or the map gets soaked), you have a backup for your safety. If for some reason you feel that you want to only use a GPS, please ensure that you have good situational awareness when you are traveling. Use of GPS is no different from the use of a cell phone in modern society: People focus too intently on the device and pay no attention to their surroundings. This lack of awareness has led to wilderness travelers getting lost, traveling through rough terrain they could have avoided, being injured or worse because they were not paying attention.

THE MOST OVERLOOKED ISSUE WITH GPS

We have experienced this personally and have seen it several times such that it warrants some focused attention here. When you first get your GPS and begin using it, the most important thing you can do is determine what the settings are. Please verify that you are using the coordinate system you wish to use. Most GPSs that are sold in the United States default to an appropriate setting. With the proliferation of online sales, including some GPSs that are shipped from overseas locations, this may not be true. Check out chapter 1 if you are unsure of what datum and grid set will be best for you and your needs. Also, your GPS receiver is much more than just something to record your track lines, or "breadcrumbs." Take this chapter and the owner's manual of your receiver outside and practice.

Image 29: Always check your settings, sometimes called preferences, in your GPS on a regular basis.

SATELLITE ISSUES

GPSs use information from satellites. This requirement means you need a good line of sight to utilize a GPS. You will improve the accuracy of the data if your GPS unit can get a line of sight to *multiple* satellites (a minimum of four). GPS units have either an external or internal antenna. These antennae have various levels of technology when it comes to their capability. If your GPS has a low-level antenna capability then you will often have difficulty getting contact on cloudy days, under heavy forest canopy or under similar widespread obstructions above you. Therefore, many GPS units do not work well indoors or under a structure with a roof (such as a pavilion or trail hut like you might find on common trails). Since satellites are not always directly overhead, your GPS will seek to connect to them at angles that are not 90 degrees to the earth. In canyons, mountainous terrain or similar areas near the bottom of a cliff face it is difficult (if not impossible) to reach these satellites. If you are having difficulty getting an accurate reading, go to the highest point you can safely and efficiently reach. Your GPS should then be able to make the line of sight to the satellites needed for better accuracy—the ideal situation is when one satellite is overhead and three others are on the horizon. Typically, GPS units are designed so that they will automatically choose the satellites that offer them the best accuracy.

GPS AND BATTERIES

Another setting within your GPS that is important to recognize is the type of battery being used. Your GPS is designed to work differently depending on the batteries that are placed in it. If you are using a lithium battery, you should switch your GPS to the lithium setting. By using the wrong setting with a particular set of batteries, you can cause issues for the circuitry within the unit.

The other common issue with GPS units and battery use is the forgetfulness of the user. Frankly, this is a problem I inflicted on myself many times before I established a routine to correct it. Always turn your GPS unit off when you do not want to use it. This step is easy to forget when you are utilizing the GPS to lay a breadcrumb trail as you travel. Make it routine to turn off your unit when you stop for a short break or for the night. Remember to turn it back on when you begin traveling again. Your GPS unit will continually send and receive signals to the satellites at intervals. Even when you are sitting and doing nothing—for example, when you camp overnight—your GPS is still sending and receiving signals, draining battery power. This is something to be mindful of and correct.

BEST PRACTICES FOR IMPROVING GPS ACCURACY

It is rather amazing that satellites 13,000 miles (20,900 km) away from Earth can communicate to a GPS receiver that I wear on my wrist. Each of the satellites orbits the earth twice per day. Many devices will give you an update on the GPS home screen or the satellite screen regarding their level of accuracy. For example, my GPS tells me as it connects to more accurate reception that the measurements are accurate to within so many feet. If, for example, that amount is 10 feet (3 m), then I know if I am looking for a specific spot that it will be within 10 feet (3 m) of where the GPS is telling me it is located. Cell phone GPS receivers are rarely less than 16 feet (5 m) off and more often approximately 65 to 98 feet (20 to 30 m) off. That is why, if you look at your position while traveling, it may show you as being off the road or trail. This is another reason I recommend getting a dedicated GPS receiver for wilderness navigation. Most often, my receiver will get me within 3 to 6 feet (1 to 2 m) of accuracy.

Here are a few ways you can help ensure that you improve the accuracy of what you receive on your device:

1. Get as clear a path to the sky as possible. Whenever possible, get your readings once you make it to the top of a mountain, hill or ridgeline. GPS receivers will contact multiple satellites. The more satellites they receive data from, the more accurate they will be. When you place yourself in a high location, you have more capability to hit satellites orbiting at various angles to Earth. Keep in mind that the satellites you are receiving from are not always directly overhead.

2. Stay away from obstructions such as tree canopies, cliff lines and vehicles. You may get a reading in a steep valley, but it will most likely be with only one satellite. If you are obtaining such readings, verify your positioning whenever you get away from the obstructions. If you are using your GPS to navigate while driving, this would include getting the GPS in the front windshield or dash area.

3. Keep a full battery and change batteries regularly. Your GPS will offer much better performance when it has a full charge.

4. Get the best antenna you can afford. Across brands, there is a wide range of names for the different antenna types. The pro of getting a powerful antenna is that it will connect to, lock on to and communicate with satellites more quickly. The antenna will also perform better in subpar conditions, such as under heavy tree canopy. The con of a high-end antenna is that it will drain the battery more quickly because it continues working in an effort to obtain or maintain signal reception with the satellites. Make sure you know how long it takes your GPS to run a set of batteries down before you plan on using it.

5. Power-saving options are important features. Power-saving modes in the GPS will tell the unit to fix on satellites less often. This makes for imperfect breadcrumb modes, but it is worth it in the end. If you do not have a power-saver mode, your GPS will constantly be looking for and locking on to satellites, which eats up precious battery life.

IMPORTANT POINTS FOR FIRST RESPONDERS

If you are a first responder, datum and grid choices are most likely determined by your administration or command staff. The standard operating procedures will differ for various agencies. If you're in a leadership position, you must verify that all GPS users on your team are utilizing the same settings. You should also know which of these settings the various other agencies you work with utilize. For best performance, all team members, associated agencies and equipment and tools must use the same settings.

USING A GPS IN CONCERT WITH A TOPO MAP

If the conditions are such that you can get good reception for your GPS, then utilizing it with a good topo map is an excellent way to stay safe and venture off the trail where it is legal to do so. A map will provide you with the ability to utilize terrain association along the way, while the GPS can be used to more accurately pinpoint your location on the map.

If you look on the edges of your map, you will see numbers that reflect the grid system on that map. The typical USGS quad map that we like to use has a combination of latitude and longitude (see image 30) and UTM (see image 31). I typically like to draw the appropriate lines on my map before I need them or when I print them off through a website or software to ensure that they are printed along with the topography.

Once you obtain your coordinates using your GPS, the gridlines then allow for a quick, easy and accurate plotting on the map. Your GPS is tracking your position and you can set waypoints as well. Each time you look at a waypoint or your current location, the GPS will show you the default coordinate system for that singular point. You can then transfer the coordinates you get on your GPS to your map for effective practice. For specifics on getting coordinates, please see the section in this chapter entitled "Waypoints." As we mentioned in chapter 1, you should read these coordinates going right, then up (page 26). Review that chapter for the section on determining your grid system.

Image 30: Latitude and longitude indicated on a map.

Image 31: UTM coordinates indicated on a map.

USING A GPS SOLO

There are several things you can do with a GPS that we will discuss in chapters 9, 10 and 11. In this section, I want to focus our attention on three important aspects of GPS use: setting waypoints, creating a track and recording a route.

SETTING WAYPOINTS

Waypoints are landmarks stored within the memory of your GPS receiver. Once a waypoint is stored, you can utilize the GPS's menu screen to pull it up and get the information you need (such as coordinates, elevation and even notes). Most GPS receivers also have a function that allows you to choose a waypoint through mapping or a menu screen then navigate to it from your current position. Keep in mind that this is a straight-shot distance and heading; it does not take into account the topography you will need to traverse. This discrepancy is another reason I recommend you carry a topography map with you to use in concert with your GPS. You will often need to travel around obstacles, so these straight-line distances and bearings must be used mostly for planning purposes—remember that often they lead to impassable areas.

You can choose waypoints to travel toward and the GPS will give you a bearing and a distance to travel to that waypoint, which is very convenient. You can find catching features (see the list on page 65) and distances to set up your pace count as well. Waypoints, catching features and distances feed off one another to help increase the accuracy of your navigation.

Waypoints can be entered into the receiver memory in one of three ways. The first is to type a set of coordinates into the GPS and save them as a waypoint (these coordinates can come from a map, or they can be given to you by another person). The second is to use your pointer or cursor on your map to highlight a point on your GPS's map and then save that point. The third way is to utilize the "mark" feature of your GPS when you are currently in a location you want to set as a waypoint. The GPS will save a waypoint on your location for later use.

CREATING A TRACK

Storing a track is nothing more than saving a series of waypoints in a sequence. Some GPS units refer to this function as "leaving breadcrumbs," as it is a more recognizable analogy for new users. When you turn this feature on in your receiver, the unit will literally keep track of your travel. Each time the receiver fixes on the satellites, it will store your location. The downside to creating a track is that it uses up a considerable amount of battery life because the GPS never turns off. The great benefit is that should you get lost, or even desire to go back the way you came into a wilderness, you can easily tell the receiver to follow the track line back out.

RECORDING A ROUTE

Recording a route is similar to creating a track in that a route is a sequence of points that are saved on your GPS receiver. The primary difference is that, typically, these routes are ones that you as the user enter when you feel it necessary—they are not automatically stored for you. When you enter a waypoint manually, you can also include a name and other notations. This allows you the ability to make waypoints more distinctive and descriptive. As an example, you might save a waypoint where you parked your vehicle, filled up your water stores and saw some wildlife. If you ever go that route again in the future, you can use that waypoint information for planning purposes.

GENERAL CHARACTERISTICS OF GPS UNITS

It would be impossible to show you each possible feature, menu or screen that you could encounter on all the GPS receivers that are currently on the market. However, there are some general characteristics that will be true for most models, so it is important that you know what those are. The following will be included in the majority of GPS units:

- **Antenna:** Most of the antennae that are available now are internal and you will never notice them. There are a few antennae that will be external and fixed to the unit itself. There are also external antennae available for many car GPS units and cell phone GPSs that are best used in a vehicle. Car GPS usage isn't the purpose of this book, but we don't want to discredit car GPS units and cell phone apps. But poor GPS signal or cell service means you may not connect to satellites well, which can lead to inaccurate readings, which can lead to life-threatening situations.

Since it is not uncommon for people to get embroiled in tragedy due to poor GPS signal in a vehicle, a more powerful antenna may help solve the problems before they arise.

• **Keypad entry:** Your keypad will take some getting used to. GPS manufacturers put a premium on screen space; therefore, GPSs will have a series of toggle buttons you can use to make choices on the screen itself. Two buttons you will often find that are set apart for this is the GoTo and Mark buttons (see image 32 of Foretrex 401). The GoTo button will give you a list of the saved waypoints. You can then choose a waypoint and travel to it as mentioned earlier. The Mark button creates a waypoint at whatever location you currently find yourself when you press it. If you are in the market for a GPS and have never owned one, look for those buttons on each model you consider while shopping—they need to be readily available for you because you will use them often. Even though the Mark button creates a waypoint at your current location, the menu options allow easy access to the info so you can change that information, allowing you to enter coordinates for a separate location that you can then navigate to. You can also choose different emojis or symbols for the points to refresh your memory regarding your waypoints. As an example, I use symbols for parking spots, edible plants, hunting tree stands and more. Doing so allows me to look at the small screen of a GPS that has a lot of waypoints mapped on it and quickly find specific points more easily.

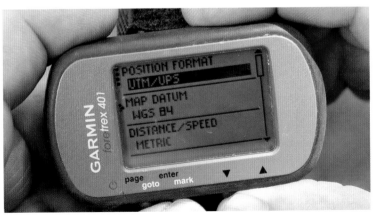

Image 32: Many controls and buttons allow quick marking of waypoints on your GPS.

- **Position screen:** This screen is the one that will give you real-time data. On many receivers, you can determine what data is on this screen so that it is customized for your needs. For example, on my position screen, I have my current location coordinates, heading and barometer reading. I can get a lot of important information at a glance.

- **Satellite screen:** This shows you how many satellites you are receiving from and their positions relative to yours. This serves to benefit you by letting you know how accurate your readings should be. Remember, four satellites or more ensures the highest accuracy.

- **Map or layout screen:** Even if your GPS receiver does not have topo maps loaded on it, you will have a map screen. This screen will be an overview that lays out any waypoints you have saved, your route and your track line if you have set it to record. On this screen, you can point toward a waypoint on the map. You can then use that to simply get info about that location or use your toggle buttons to go to that location.

- **Settings:** I believe it is worth your time to check your settings each time you go out. Doing so will ensure that you're using the datum set you want to be using. Once you get used to using a coordinate system, you will most likely recognize it quickly. As we noted in chapter 1, the coordinates all have a certain number of digits and other identifiers to each of them.

OTHER USEFUL TECHNOLOGICAL EQUIPMENT

If everything in the wilderness worked the way it is supposed to, a GPS receiver with integrated map, compass, barometer and altimeter would get nearly all jobs done that we would need for wilderness navigation. That is why I have dedicated so much space to GPS technology in this chapter. A GPS is one piece of equipment that I feel is a worthwhile investment in technology. I hope it has also been made clear that there are several things that can go wrong with them. It should additionally be clear that to understand GPS usage, you should be well grounded in map and compass skills *first*. That is why we put these first three chapters in the order you currently find them: They are a natural progression into wilderness navigation.

If you ask any instructor of outdoor skills what the best methodology is for teaching students, they will give some variation of, "Teach them in stages." We all put our thoughts and experiences in a file folder called the brain as we learn. If we put too much into the file folder at one time, it is in disarray and the information is hard to recall. Please understand that chapters 1 and 2 cover the building blocks of things you will need to do land navigation right. In this rest of this chapter, we want to consider some items that may be used on a more advanced level, especially as it relates to working or communicating with others for wilderness navigation.

ALTIMETER

An altimeter is one of those items that enhances your ability to determine your position on your map. It gives you your elevation anytime you need it. It is a great device to have if you are adventuring in landscape that has a wide range of elevation changes. For many years, to use an altimeter would require you to carry a separate tool to determine your elevation. When ounces equal pounds, the altimeter was something that often got left behind, since a map and compass (and the requisite skill to use them) could do most of that work for you. Now that altimeters are an included part of most GPS receivers and many outdoor sports watches (see the sidebar on page 92), we can easily refer to them without carrying an extra item. We should know how to use an altimeter to benefit our quality control during wilderness navigation.

USING AN ALTIMETER ON THE TRAIL

Look at the following (image 33). If you traveling on trail X and reference your altimeter, you will find that you have an elevation reading of 1300. By knowing you are on that trail and knowing your elevation, you can pinpoint your location on the map rather easily.

USING AN ALTIMETER OFF THE TRAIL

If you go off-trail and travel along a recognizable feature, you can also pinpoint your location. This feature can be a spur, ridgeline or valley. At some point, each of these features will have a descending or ascending slope to them. If you can locate yourself on the map before you start traveling and go along one of these slopes, you may not be able to recognize where you are. This could be because of heavy vegetation, obstructions that move you off a direct line, your having forgotten to do your pace count, cloudy conditions or darkness. You will not be able to see terrain features well. By using your altimeter, you can find your location as you proceed along your route.

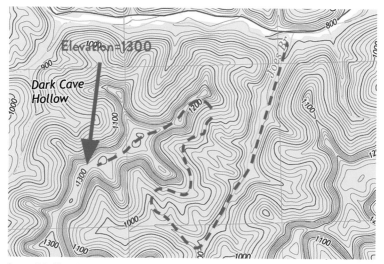

Image 33: Knowing your elevation can help you find the contour you are traveling.

USING AN ALTIMETER TO FOLLOW A CONTOUR

There are several reasons you may want to follow a specific contour along a mountain or hill, depending on who you are:

- **If you are a hiker or backpacker:** If there are obstructions along a trail and you divert but do not want to get lost, you can follow a contour for a while, then make your way back to your original route.

- **If you are a forester:** You can cruise a steep elevation to do a timber survey.

- **If you are a naturalist:** You can follow a contour to make an orderly search of various plant species.

- **If you are a biologist:** You can follow a contour while surveying an elevation for nesting sites of various species of animals.

If you do follow a contour without an altimeter, you will find it is rather natural for you to drift downhill no matter how hard you try to stay at the same elevation. The altimeter can keep you on track to avoid this drift.

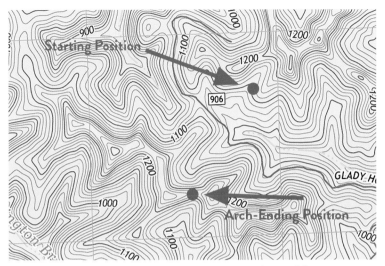

Image 34: Use your altimeter to avoid drifting downhill on exploration hikes.

An altimeter can also be used to find a good route to a specific location on your map. For example, see image 34. On this image, you will see a natural arch. You will notice that walking directly up or down to it is going to be difficult walking. If you climb the hill to its known elevation, then you can follow a contour around until you get to your desired location.

SATELLITE MESSENGERS

Satellite messengers are devices born out of similar technology found in personal locator beacons. These handheld devices are a way to communicate to others via text messages in areas where there is no cell phone capability.

Satellite messengers are designed to transmit either a very short text message or location coordinates to recipients of your choosing. We have seen modern explorers who set these devices to send information back to their social media platforms. This allows supporters or financiers of explorations to get regular updates of how it's going.

OUTDOOR AND ADVENTURE WATCHES

Technology is evolving quickly when it comes to how small a device can be to boost navigation aids. Cell phone apps are so user-friendly that they are the most affordable way for companies to get such aids to market. Smaller still, watches pack quite a punch when it comes to navigation and other outdoor aids. Following is a list of a few watches to check out. These watches run within a wide range of prices (the prices listed are approximate). While many of these prices seem high, users must consider that some of these models can be used as a GPS, compass and fitness tracker. This may eliminate the need to buy various pieces to accomplish these tasks. The watches are listed here in alphabetical order:

1. Casio PRW2500T-7 ($400): This watch has no GPS but it does have a barometer, altimeter and compass.

2. Garmin epix ($549): This watch offers GPS and mapping.

3. Garmin fēnix ($549): This is a very high-quality GPS-enabled device.

4. Suunto Spartan Sport ($385): This is another high-quality GPS-enabled device with activity tracking.

5. Suunto Traverse ($293): This watch has GPS and can sync with smartphones.

Image 35: Many brands of watches have GPS and compass features on them.

What is interesting about satellite messengers is that they do not utilize any governmental satellite networks. Rather, using these devices requires a regular subscription fee. It is important to note that different services offer various plans. Those plans will determine the interval at which devices track you. This range goes from a few hours to minutes. Those that track you every few minutes are much more expensive. Currently, the technology and power that these devices use require you to have a view to an open sky to transmit to the satellites.

The obvious benefit of these devices is that those who are connected to you can track you for peace of mind. The transmission feature allows you to send preprogrammed messages such as "All is OK" or similar updates. There are various brands and models, but most of them also have an emergency button that requires you to go through more than a single step to activate so you do not hit the emergency signal by accident.

TWO-WAY RADIOS

Cell phone technology is advancing at a rapid pace and can often be used in many wilderness areas. However, there are still many reasons why two-way radios are a good choice for backcountry excursions:

- Many backcountry areas do not have cell phone tower coverage.

- Two-ways typically last longer on the initial set of batteries and batteries can be easily replaced.

- Some GPS units have two-way capability so you have both technology pieces wrapped up in one.

- Search-and-rescue teams operate on frequencies that can be reached by other radios. Therefore, when you are within their usable distance, two-way radios can be used when you have no ability to make a call.

- They are a backup method to getting accurate weather data from NOAA.

HAM RADIO

Hertz-Armstrong-Marconi: Sounds like a law firm, doesn't it? Actually, it's the spelled-out name for HAM radios. HAM radio licensure allows the user to access radio towers that the average citizen can't. We are both HAM radio operators and enjoy the practice of utilizing them. With training, practice, certification and understanding of how the HAM system operates, you can literally talk around the world with a HAM radio. For more information, consult the American Relay Radio League's website at www.arrl.org.

There are many helpful hints that will make your experience with two-way radios an optimal one:

- Ignore the "will travel 25 miles (40 km)" marketing tricks on the typical handheld radio. Most will travel 2 miles (3 km) or less, and that is heavily dependent on terrain.

- Some features that do not allow good radio communication are deep valleys, tall formations, heavily forested areas and hills. Radio waves travel primarily in straight lines, so they will not go up and over or around an obstruction. The interesting sidenote to this is some sheer obstructions, such as a cliff face, will actually "bounce" a radio signal off of it. This will allow you to sometimes send a signal in a different direction than that of a straight line to another radio.

- Obtain a high point whenever possible to ensure good radio transmission.

- Attaching a radio to your pack away from your body will benefit it. Your body will sometimes negatively affect its ability to receive signal.

- If you are not using your radio on a regular basis, you can store the radio and batteries separate and only put them together in an emergency.

Radios that are designed to be utilized in the United States work on two frequencies: Family Radio Service (FRS) or General Mobile Radio Service (GMRS). It is illegal to use these radios outside North America. GMRS used to require a small license fee to legally use it. Due to its widespread use, however, there is no longer a fee.

TWO-WAY RADIO ETIQUETTE

Unlike telephones, you cannot talk over another person on a radio transmission. This necessitates using good communication etiquette so the transmission is not a jumbled mess. Proper etiquette also ensures that you are heard and that you can hear others fully. Here are some helpful hints to facilitate this clear radio communication:

1. Have your message prepared before you initiate transmission. Airwaves are controlled by the unit that has more power. Only one person can talk at any given time. Remember that plain talk is always better than tactical-type phrasing or commands (i.e., like those used in the military and in law enforcement). In that job structure tactical phrasing is imperative, but for regular adventurers simple language is best.

2. When you press the button to talk, wait a minimum of one second before speaking. This allows adequate time for the radios to connect before talking so no information is missing in transmission.

3. Identify yourself and the person (or people) you wish to speak to. If another party has a similar system, they can be on the same channel and think you are speaking to them. This identification helps prevent confusion.

4. Tell everyone you are finished with a transmission, even if you know the conversation will go longer. You can do this by saying, "Over." This lets the person on the other end of the conversation know you are finished and that it is their turn to talk.

5. Wait until you are certain the other party does not wish to transmit. You can ask if they received the message with, "How copy?" or "Did you get that?"

6. Let the other party know if you need more time to respond. If you are asked a question and need to process information (e.g., to determine grid coordinates), let the other party know you received the question and are determining the answer by saying, "Stand by."

7. When you have completed a conversation, repeat your name and say, "Out." This lets the other party know you are done and not in the transmission at that point.

TROUBLESHOOTING: OVERCOMING COMMON PROBLEMS WITH TECHNOLOGY

In detailing the functions and usefulness of GPS units, I have attempted to show you how to best use them. Some of the problematic items that we see regularly are listed here. Many of these have been covered earlier in the chapter, so use the following information as a refresher:

- Upon getting a GPS for the first time, or upon recognizing the importance of its settings for the first time, check the units that your GPS is set to. You should change to whatever units that you are comfortable with, that match your preferred map, that your team uses and so on.

- Make time to get familiar with your unit before ever taking it afield and needing it for navigation. This should include setting a few waypoints, laying a trail and more around your home or a park. In this manner, you can get used to the fundamentals before your navigation in the wilderness is dependent on your GPS.

- Do not try to get important information from your unit within the first few minutes of turning it on. A GPS is not like a cell phone. It will take much longer to connect to the satellites and start receiving information. I typically do a check to see how many satellites I am connected to, hoping for a minimum of four, before I start using the unit.

- Keep in mind that the satellites you are wanting to connect to are not always directly overhead. Also note that the more satellites you connect with, the better. And access to satellites at different angles is preferable. Therefore, when seeking good reception, choose sights that have a clear path to the sky in multiple directions whenever possible.

- It seems simple, but as I get older, I recognize that both my compass and GPS are hard to read without glasses. Don't forget that you may need them to see your equipment properly.

- An altimeter can be a reference item or one that you use along a hike. Get an altimeter that can be easily accessed. Drifting down a hill is easy to do, especially on a steep incline—regularly referencing it is imperative.

- Radio communication is sketchy at best. Always make plans with those you are adventuring with regarding what to do if you lose all cell and radio connection. Designating big events in windows of time is one way of doing this. For example, establish with your group that if you happen to lose communication you will meet at a certain location. If that window is not met, then necessary steps (such as possibly contacting search and rescue) can be taken.

- Sports watches that contain all the valuable technology are a great way to carry a lot of tools in one small package. However, you should always carry battery backup and take the necessary steps throughout your adventure to protect the screen. Many military-grade watches are made to handle a lot of abuse, but your typical watch used for recreational exercise may not be as hardy.

It bears repeating: Technology is great but will ultimately fail. Keep working on your map and compass skills so they stay sharp. Pick up some of these other pieces of equipment to enhance your skill set. We recommend that you not become dependent on technology alone. By understanding map and compass skills, you will always have a great backup plan, and those skills only enhance your ability to use technology to its fullest capability.

If everything does go wrong and you need to be rescued, we want you to be able to have a basic skill set to help you get home safely. In the following chapter, we will help you help yourself in the event you have a multilevel failure of skills or equipment.

QUESTIONS FOR PRACTICE

1. Look at the map supplied with this book. What datum set and coordinate system can you use to coordinate with your GPS?

2. True or false: A huge benefit of a GPS unit is that it allows you to avoid the hassle of taking and using a paper map.

3. What are the two major issues that might impede the effectiveness of your GPS?

4. What is the single set of coordinates you mark with your GPS generally called?

5. List at least one thing you can do to increase the number of satellites your GPS receiver will connect to.

6. True or false: Any type of battery will work fine with most GPS units.

7. True or false: You should always verify the factory setting of a new GPS unit.

8. How many satellites are required to get a quality level of accuracy?

9. True or false: When seeking satellite reception, the best satellite to connect to for accuracy is directly overhead.

10. Can you convert from Lat/Long to the UTM grid system using only your GPS?

Answers: (1) WGS 84 datum; NAD 83 datum; Lat/Long or UTM grid system. (2) False. (3) Battery life and satellite connection. (4) A waypoint. (5) Be in unobstructed and open space, go to a higher elevation, have a stronger antenna. (6) False. The GPS and battery types must match. (7) True. (8) Four or more. (9) False. It is best to connect to multiple satellites at angles steeper than your position. (10) Yes. Save a waypoint and then change the settings to the grid system to see the new grid system coordinates.

GET OUT AND PRACTICE

I am excited for you. We now get to add one more piece of quality control for wilderness navigation use to our practice. I am going to do this one a little differently. Now that we have a good understanding of maps, compasses and GPS units, I am going to ask you to use your enclosed map for this practice. You have probably noticed that I am adding some more difficulties for you as we move along. Using a map of an unfamiliar area will present extra challenges for you, which I am sure you will be able to overcome.

❏ Get your GPS unit (or open a cell phone app) and the enclosed map. Look in the lower left corner of the map and find where it states the datum and grid system being used on the map. The datum is WGS 84/NAD 83, and the grid is UTM. Adjust your GPS settings or verify that your GPS unit is on those settings.

❏ Find Leatherwood Creek on your map. Find where Glady Branch flows into it. Let's assume you park on the road at Leatherwood and hike along the creek (there is no trail) to the end of Glady Branch. Here are some things you should be able to do at this point and that make for good practice:

  ❏ Find the UTM coordinates of your starting point, which will be where you park.

  ❏ Find the UTM coordinates where Glady Branch ends on the map.

  ❏ Use the scale of the map to determine the approximate distance of your hike.

  ❏ Use your GPS to find a straight-line distance between the two points. Note how this is most likely different from the measurement you got using the scale.

  ❏ When you get to the spot where the Glady Branch starts (away from where it flows into Leatherwood Creek), there will be something directly in front of you. Use your map to determine if that is a steep hill, lake or open field.

  ❏ Determine in what general direction you will be traveling if you walk along this creek.

- Use your GPS unit to convert your coordinates from UTM into Lat/Long. After doing so, look at the Lat/Long references along the bottom and side of the map to see how your coordinates relate to the map.

- Assume a friend of yours found an endangered American chestnut tree. You are a big fan of trees and know this is a very interesting find, so you would like to see it as well. Your friend gives you the coordinates, which correspond to a place on the enclosed map. The following is a list of questions and considerations you should think about when looking for the tree:

  - The coordinates are 17S 277315 4213086. What system are they, and does your map show those coordinates?

  - What sort of land feature do you find at this location that will help you find the tree you are looking for? You will be using terrain association as you get close to the location to verify the spot.

  - There are three possible routes to this location. Look at these to see some pros and cons of each:

    - The first route (which is also the most direct) travels on the lake to the area in which the two large hollows start. This is an option if you are a paddler, but let's assume you want to hike to your destination.

    - The second route would start by driving east on Leatherwood Road until you came to a spot due south of the coordinates given. By looking at the map, you could predetermine coordinates and enter them into your GPS unit. You could also look at the area terrain features. By using both these methods, you would have a good estimate as you were driving on where to park and head out on your hike. Going this route is the quickest way on foot. It presents some very steep terrain to get to the tree.

    - The third route is probably the easiest in terms of terrain to walk, but it is also the longest. This is not an issue if you have plenty of time and enjoy getting out in nature. You could drive and park at the intersection of Buck Creek and the road that branches to the north of Leatherwood Creek Road. You would then have a relatively easy hike on slowly descending terrain along Buck Creek. Much like the second route, you could enter in the waypoint data and pay attention to the terrain on the map. Once you get close to a position north of the coordinates, you could walk up the hill and to the saddle where the tree is located.

☐ Let's assume now that your GPS unit fails right after you leave the vehicle. What sort of things must you do to navigate with only map and compass? Here are a few that come to mind:

   ☐ Terrain association is going to be key. As you walk, you need to count the hollows along each of the routes to make sure you are in the right spot.

   ☐ You should log the key terrain features in a journal along the way, both by vehicle or by foot, to verify these spots.

   ☐ Once you come to the location in which you want to head directly to the tree, you'll use your compass to take a bearing. You would verify that the direction coincides with the features on the map (don't forget to calculate declination).

   ☐ Look at the bottom of the map near center-left to see the declination diagram. Your declination is 6°16' at this location. (I will typically round to 6 degrees when traveling on this map.)

There are a few ways to utilize all that we have studied together thus far. It is my hope that are you beginning to see a few things. I will point them out here in case you need a little help.

A map is the most important tool in wilderness navigation. When you add a compass, it takes some of the guesswork out of map orientation. It also adds a significant level of quality assurance when doing your terrain association. GPS use is one more step above that in quality assurance. When your GPS is working correctly, it will give you near-pinpoint accuracy for your position on the earth. This serves to quickly determine your position on a map so you can continue or change direction when needed.

There are a few other items that will help you increase the quality of the wilderness navigation puzzle. I will cover them in the next chapter and challenge you with some practical exercises that use all the common tools at our disposal.

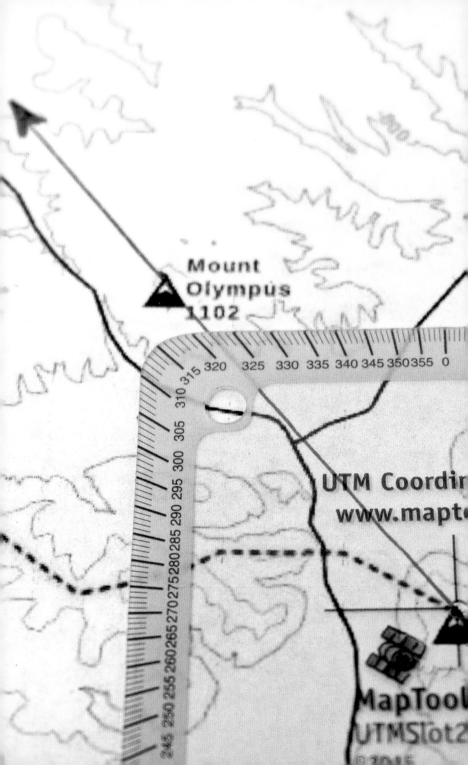

Mount
Olympus
1102

315 320 325 330 335 340 345 350 355 0
310
305
300
295
290
285
280
275
270
265
260
255
250
245

UTM Coordin
www.mapt

MapTool
UTMSlot2

CHAPTER 4

OTHER ITEMS YOU NEED TO DO LAND NAVIGATION RIGHT OR TO LOOK COOL (OR BOTH)

If you think adventure is dangerous, try routine—
it's lethal. —Paulo Coelho

It is a wonderful thing when an accomplished wilderness navigator can assist lost hikers using technology. Tracy has completed some variation of this several times in his role as a search-and-rescue volunteer.

On one such occasion, a 911 call was received saying that two hikers had called and were on a trail but unsure of which direction to get to their vehicle. In this case, they had cell coverage and had dialed 911 to seek help. Dispatchers contacted the local search-and-rescue team Tracy is on. He was able to make cell phone contact with the hikers. Although there are many SAR events that require personal assistance, this one was going to be accomplished with technology. After contact was made with the lost hikers, Tracy was able to send a text to them. By responding to the text, he was able to get the lost hikers' coordinates. Tracy then utilized his Gaia app to find their location in the region. With the overview provided by the app, he was able to tell the hikers which direction to go on the nearest trail and how far away they were from the parking lot. He then advised them to take a screenshot of the standard compass app (image 36) on their phone every few minutes. The app contains their coordinates in latitude and longitude. Although we typically use a metric system, this sort of conversion is very easy to do on an app. Tracy could then remotely verify that they were continuing in the right direction and guide them back to the relative safety of their vehicle.

We assigned this chapter the title it has for good reason. I have seen our students at Nature Reliance School come to class with a wide range of gear options to help with wilderness navigation, most of which they have not known how to use. Outside of the obvious items I have discussed thus far (i.e., map, compass, GPS), there are many other items that will assist you in your efforts toward proper wilderness navigation. For those of you who have this gear but don't know how to use it, this chapter is for you.

You may have noted that while I am a fan of technology, I do not like being dependent on it in the wilderness. There should always be methods to take care of your needs and wants without it. Technology items are more like comfort items in your otherwise usable skill set in the outdoors. GPS receivers offer the user the ability to measure how much they have walked without the need for a map or compass. You can also measure distances on a map with solid terrain association skills that we helped you develop in chapter 1. You may wonder how to do that systematically if none of those items are available. There are some simple tips and gear pieces we can use to help us estimate the distance traveled. It will require a small amount of work on your part before you need this skill.

Image 36: The fundamental compass app on most phones will oftentimes give latitude and longitude. We recommend not relying on them for accurate compass use.

PROTRACTORS, SCALES AND OTHER MEASURING TOOLS

If you are new to wilderness navigation and you just read the word *protractor* in the title of this section, don't worry—we are not going back to elementary school math class. *Protractor* is the most common word used to describe a tool that you place on the map to assist in determining coordinates, distances and more (see image 37). You can make your own, but at Nature Reliance School we use tools made by MapTools (you can find them at maptools.com). You will hear these items being called protractors, grid scales, grid squares, slot tools, grid tools, pocket tools and by the trade name MapTools. The key is that these

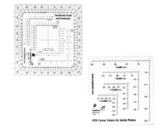

Image 37: Map protractors come in a wide array of sizes, scales, uses and styles of use.

Image 38: Some map tools will have multiple scales on them.

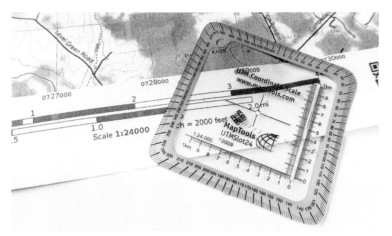

Image 39: You must match your protractor to the scale of the map you are using.

tools (image 38) represent a metric measurement and scale. If you know what the scale of your map is then you can use a map tool with the same scale to assist you in determining coordinates, angles and points of intersection.

Take time to review or recall the explanation of grid systems in chapter 1. Excluding that Lat/Long system, each of those squares appearing on a map are representations of a metric measurement. Since each of those squares is the same size, you can find a protractor that corresponds to it (see image 39). You can use the protractor to determine more exact coordinates and then input them into a GPS, share them over a radio or record them for later use.

MEASUREMENT WITH YOUR PROTRACTOR

We teach protractor use in our wilderness navigation coursework. Many people find it hard to understand, while others never again use their compass to determine angles after learning it.

If you look at a map protractor closely, you will see that around the edge there are numbers going from 0 to 360. You guessed it—that matches the degrees on your compass. Follow these steps to get an accurate grid bearing using only your protractor:

1. Draw a line from your starting point to your ending point.

2. Note the small hole in the center of the protractor. Place that small hole directly over the starting point.

3. Line up the lines of the protractor with the grid lines of your map.

4. Note where the line you drew crosses the edge of the protractor and the corresponding number that goes with it. That is your grid bearing on the map.

5. If you need to use this on your compass, do not forget to calculate in your declination.

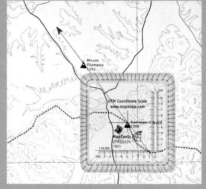

Image 40: You can use a protractor to determine the azimuth amount on your map. Remember that you must adjust for declination when taking that amount to your compass.

There are many different styles of protractors (image 41). The following are the ones that our students seem to find easiest to use. When we teach a class, we share some of each for the students to practice with. They keep coming back to one of these three as their favorite:

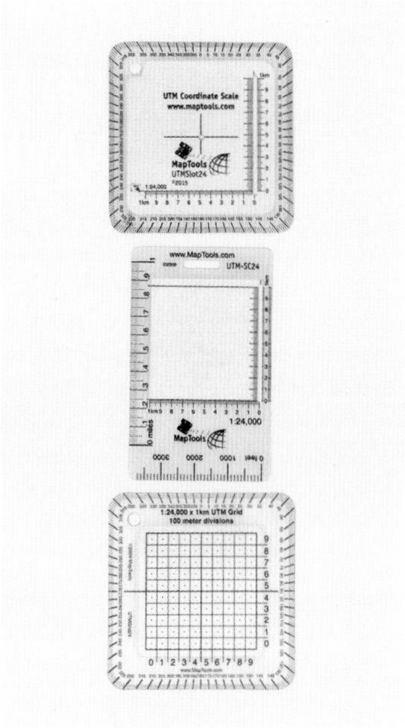

- **Slot:** This kind is slightly different but easier to determine coordinates with, in our opinion. You will notice the small slot on the protractor. You put this on the location you want to determine coordinates for, or you use coordinates you already have on the scale, and use your pencil to mark the spot through the slot. This access to the map makes it easy to leave a waypoint mark where you need it to be.

Image 41: Each of these protractors is the same scale. You can find one that meets your individual needs and wants. Pictured are a slot, grid and full grid protractors.

- **Full Grid:** This type correlates directly to the grid squares on your map. You place the outermost boundary of the protractor directly on top of the lines of the coordinate grid square of your map.

- **Mini corner:** These are the smallest and lightest protractor options available. With these protractors, you place the right-angle point on the point you want to determine coordinates for (not pictured in image 41).

INCREASING YOUR SITUATIONAL AWARENESS FOR WILDERNESS NAVIGATION

One of the largest misconceptions about "survival" training is that it is a reactive practice of dealing with a tragedy or stressful event after it happens. Our perspective is very different. We consistently focus our attention on ways for you to be situationally aware, so you can be proactive instead. It is much better to see dangers or problems before they happen, so you can adjust your actions or location. Here are some simple tips to help you increase your situational awareness for wilderness navigation:

1. Always look ahead at the route you are walking, and look ahead on the map as well, so you know what to expect.

2. Regularly look back from where you have come from. If you need to turn around and walk back, you will be familiar with your surroundings. Pay attention to notable landmarks, plants or trees that stand out so you will recognize them on the return trip.

3. Know what time it is and how much time you have left before nightfall.

4. Pay attention to the weather and do not disregard it.

5. Communicate regularly with everyone in your group. Whether that is a party of two or twenty is of no consequence. By communicating regularly, you can find out early if someone is ill or injured. Taking the necessary precautions early will keep these situations tenable.

PACE COUNT

The practice of developing a pace count is a way that you can determine the distance into a wilderness by counting your steps, or paces. For reference, we use the metric system for our students. This is because we recommend using the UTM grid system or one of its variants. By having a pace count that's based in meters, you can directly correlate your information to the map and its grid squares. Follow these simple steps:

- To get started, measure a straight-line distance of 330 feet (100 m). Mark the beginning and ending point of this distance. For your first time, we recommend something on flat, level ground without any obstructions.

- Start walking along the line before the starting point and walk along the line. Once you step across the starting line, begin counting your steps. Walk as naturally as possible along the straight line and go past the ending point.

- As soon as you get past the ending point, stop counting steps. The number of steps you took is your pace count for 330 feet (100 m).

- For simplicity's sake, most people will only count one foot (I use the left), so they do not have to count every single step they take. For example, my pace count for 330 feet (100 m) is 70. This means that for me to walk 330 feet (100 m), my left foot would contact the ground 70 times.

If you are new to using pace count, it will be bothersome while you start practicing with it. It will seem as if you are doing nothing more than counting while you are out. Once you get used to counting paces, it will become second nature. Now that I have been using pace count for many years, it has become more of an estimate than anything else. I actually know how much effort and time goes into a distance approximate to 330 feet (100 m). I can then keep up with my very approximated distance. Keep in mind that pace count is not something you will be using on its own. At minimum, you will also rely on your compass bearing and terrain association. You can easily include a logbook to bring all these pieces together for quality assurance. Developing your pace count is a critical step to finding yourself during a self-rescue.

Now that you have your pace count, the obvious question is, how do we go about using it? This is where a little math is going to come into play.

Let's assume that you are walking on a flat, level trail that has no obstructions. We'll use my pace count as an example. As I begin walking, I count as my left foot hits the ground each time. Once I reach my pace count number of 70, I know I have walked 330 feet (100 m). This is not an exact measurement, but experience tells me it is a very close approximation.

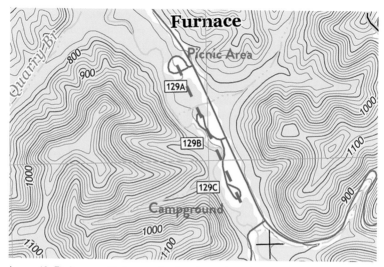

Image 42: Find measurable features in a location to determine a pace count.

To use this practically, pull out the enclosed map. Look at image 42. Let's use something easy to help us develop our pace count. You will notice that to go from the picnic area of Clear Creek (the large circle) to the southeastern loop of the campground is approximately 330 feet (100 m) using the scale at the bottom of the map. By knowing that my pace count is 70, it would be easy for me to walk from the picnic area to that end of the campground in approximately 70 paces. The ground is relatively flat, and there should not be a lot of barriers. You can apply this in any scenario you wish to put yourself into during wilderness treks. Here are a few examples:

• You are on a trail hike and know there is a berry patch that is 990 feet (300 m) into the trail and about 165 feet (50 m) east of the trail at that point. Obviously, you can use a GPS, but if you don't have one you can use your pace count to get to your favorite berry patch.

• You have to navigate around an object. We will do this in the practical exercises at the end of this chapter.

• You need to leave a trail to use the bathroom. Most recommendations say to move a minimum of 200 feet (60 m) off the trail to do this. Using your compass, you can head off the trail at a known heading and walk out your expected pace count for 200 feet (60 m). When you are done, you come back the reverse bearing and the same pace count to get back to the trail. This simple exercise could save your life (reread the opening story of chapter 1).

- You want to do a search for something that's been lost or a nesting site on the ground in the wilderness. You can use your compass to turn 90 degrees and the same pace count to create a box around an area. Shorten your steps and work your way into the center of the box. This sort of practice is covered in-depth in chapter 8.

Those in dedicated infantry units such as you find in the US Marines or US Army will often develop their pace count several times. This will include trekking over flat ground, going uphill, going downhill, moving through thick terrain, carrying a heavy pack on and so forth. This practice allows them to be very comfortable and accurate no matter what the situation.

That much practice may be a bit of overkill for those of us who are weekend adventurers, but it is a possibility if our adventures called for it. Now that we understand how a pace count works, we can also understand how pace count beads (aka Ranger beads; see image 43) work. The hardest part of utilizing a pace count is keeping up with how far you have traveled. These beads take some of that confusion away. Pace count beads are an easy way to keep track. Every time you walk 330 feet (100 m), pull one of the bottom beads down. You will note that there are nine beads. Once you have pulled down all nine beads, you have walked 2,970 feet (900 m). When you travel the next 330 feet (100 m), pull one of the top beads down and start the bottom beads over again. In this manner, it is easier for you to keep track with how far you have walked.

Image 43: Pace count, aka Ranger beads, will help you keep track of your distance walked. On this set, you can see that one bead pulled up top equals 1 kilometer and two beads pulled on the bottom equals 200 meters for a total travel distance of 1,200 meters.

This same task can be completed by using something other than pace count beads. A friend of mine, whom I worked with on a survey crew, would make marks on survey stakes as we walked along to keep track of approximate distances. Another person I read about would keep small stones in his pocket and pull a stone out of one pocket and put it in the other every 330 feet (100 m). It doesn't matter how you go about keeping up with the count—just do it. In our estimation, pace count beads are an efficient way of doing that.

There are a number of things that will affect your pace count. Keep these in mind as you develop yours and continue to use it in various conditions:

- **Angle of a slope:** Your pace count will change on both downhill and uphill hikes.

- **Weather:** Uncomfortable conditions such as rain, snow or ice will cause a navigator to shorten their pace.

- **Windy conditions:** If strong winds are hitting you in the face, your pace will shorten. If the wind is hitting you from behind, your pace will lengthen.

- **Pack and gear:** The more you carry, the shorter your pace.

- **Strata:** If the surfaces you are walking on are loose, your pace will shorten.

- **Low or no visibility:** Your pace will shorten if you are not able to see where you are walking.

- **Running:** If you are moving quickly, your pace will lengthen.

During the writing of this book, I assisted in teaching a man-tracking course that included a sniper-spotter pair from the US Marine Corps. These men are some of the world's best at using technology, skill and a strong will to accomplish dangerous missions around the world. One of the most useful skills that you can gain from such people is the ability to estimate distance. While a rangefinder can give you an incredibly accurate reading, you can easily use some basic observation skills to judge distance.

ESTIMATING ANGLES AND DISTANCE

When you are located in an area that offers a visual to the horizon, utilizing your fingers can assist you in determining the angles between objects in front of you. As you might imagine, this is only an approximation. Whenever more accurate methods are available (such as using your compass), employ them. If you need to use your fingers, however, follow these guidelines:

1. Each finger in front of your eyes on your outstretched arm represents approximately 2 degrees. Therefore, if you have three fingers in front of you measuring the distance between two hills or peaks there are 6 degrees difference between the two peaks.

2. A fist will represent 8 degrees of distance between the two.

3. The approximate distance from your outstretched thumb and forefinger is 15 degrees.

4. The approximate distance from your outstretched "aloha" (thumb and little finger) is 20 degrees.

Image 44: Each finger represents an approximate 2°. In this, there is an approximate 8° difference between the two hills in the distance.

The following are ways that we have been taught to judge distance:

- At a distance of 5 miles (8 km), you can recognize most buildings.

- At a distance of 2 miles (3 km), you will recognize that vehicles are moving.

- At a distance of 1 mile (1.5 km), the human form will appear as a dot. Trees appear as nothing more than a clump.

- At a distance of ½ mile (805 m), the human form will appear like a fence post. There is no ability to distinguish between arms or legs. Rather than a clump, large branches of trees can be seen, as can their individual trunks if they are isolated rather than in a forest.

- At a distance of 250 yards (230 m), you will start to see the human face. Arms and hands can be seen when they are away from the core.

- At a distance of 100 yards (90 m), you will see a human's eyes and discern individual leaves on an isolated tree.

- At a distance of 50 yards (45 m), you can see the eyes of a person. Individual leaves can be discerned on a tree, even in a forest. Individual tree trunks can also be recognized.

The preceding tips are all great methods of estimating distance, but there can be many problems to hamper this process, including the following:

- Proper sunlight is essential to measure accurately. If there is little light, items will seem farther away. If items have lots of sunlight on them, they will appear closer.

- If you are in an open, flat area things will appear closer than they are. This is because they are small in comparison to the environment around them.

- If you are in an area with limited or channeled vision (such as a gorge or forest road), the items you are seeing will appear farther away than they are.

- In our examples in the preceding list, note how difficult it is to distinguish individual leaves. This is because they blend in with the background and other leaves surrounding them. Items that blend in with their background will appear farther away than they actually are.

TIME COUNT

Another way of estimating distance without map tools is to note a known distance and determine how long it takes you to walk it. This is a very common method for backpackers and through-hikers to keep up with their distances while hiking. Ask any regular hiker how many miles they can walk in eight hours, and they will be able to tell you. They will also most likely tell you it depends on the terrain. Eight hours of hiking up a mountainside in the Rocky Mountains is vastly different than eight hours walking up and down hills in my home state of Kentucky. The only equipment you need for doing this is a good watch (or cell phone clock). You can also do a time count by estimating the time of day, utilizing the sun. There will be more of that in chapter 6.

ESTIMATING YOUR TIME BEFORE SUNSET

Being able to know how much time you have before the sun sets is an important aspect of wilderness adventure. With ample use of cell phones and watches, knowing the approximate time you have left before sundown is only a matter of paying attention to the previous day's sun. As with all things outdoors, we like to consider what to do when your gear, especially electronic gear, fails. You can estimate the time before sunset rather easily by doing the following steps:

1. Place yourself in such a place that you see both the sun and the horizon. You can estimate the horizon if you have a hill directly in front of you.

2. Stretch your arm in front of your face and turn your fingers 90 degrees to the palm of your hand.

3. Place the bottom finger as if it were laying on the horizon that is in front of you.

4. Count up your fingers to see how many it takes for them to be directly under the sun in your line of sight.

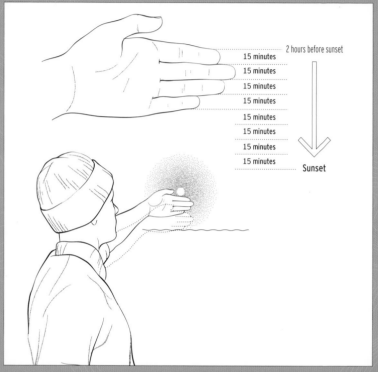

Image 45: Each finger represents fifteen minutes of time left before sunset. In this illustration, you have two hours.

5. Each finger represents approximately fifteen minutes of time before the sun sets. Essentially, one hand is equal to one hour of remaining sunlight. This means if the sun is on top of your third finger, you have forty-five minutes of sunlight left.

6. You can stack your hands on top of each other to get times greater than one hour.

PEDOMETERS

Nearly every cell phone available today has some sort of step tracker that comes with it. These are great for exercise. They are also good for approximating distance in the wilderness. As mentioned earlier, your wilderness pace count is likely going to be different than your everyday pace count, so it is in your interest to get an accurate step-distance count in the wilderness areas you like to visit. This should also give you the opportunity to see how accurate your cell phone reception is in the areas you frequent. As with all things related to cell phones, the phone is accurate only when it is receiving information from cell towers. I ruck for exercise several times a week and sometimes I wear a heart-rate monitor and step tracker. There are sections where I ruck that do not get good cell service. The route that gets plotted out for me on my app will indicate straight-line distance from where I lose cell coverage to where I pick it up again. The time between is nowhere near straight-line distance.

The old-school pedometers that attach to your shoe or belt are likely to be more accurate than a cell phone because they do not require cell service. Although this is one more thing to pack, I think they add value to a good hike. They help you set goals on trips to motivate you to keep moving forward (see the sidebar on page 118).

ALTIMETERS

Altimeters are indispensable additions to those who regularly use wilderness navigation skills. They allow you to determine your elevation rather easily. When you use an altimeter in concert with a map, you can pinpoint your location along a known route, navigate along a contour or avoid an obstruction. We take you through some practical applications of altimeters in chapter 3.

LIGHT SOURCES

I believe that a light source is one of the items you should include in the equipment you carry every day. There are some things about flashlights that are useful for wilderness navigators to understand. You will often need a light during navigation if you are in an area where there is heavy tree cover (and, obviously, when you need to navigate in the dark). Even in heavy tree cover, the details of both the map and compass are sometimes hard to see, making a good light source invaluable.

GOAL SETTING WHEN HIKING FOR ENJOYMENT OR EXERCISE

I have the good fortune that part of my work is to consult with gear manufacturers and sellers for prototypes and similar reviews. Some of that gear is hiking or rucking related. I spend time several times per week hiking and wearing different packs, rain gear, boots, pants and other items. It is definitely fun but I admit that sometimes it gets old. I have several ways I use wilderness navigation skills and gear to continue when I wake up "not feeling it." I am sure you can adapt some of the following tips to whatever you like to do in the outdoors (please note that most of these are done using a map that is more detailed than what a 1:24000 scale can provide):

1. I keep my cell phone with me to count my steps. If I am testing out a series of packs, I will tell myself that I must walk a certain number of steps with each pack.

2. I use my GPS to track myself. I keep a timer handy and have it set to ten minutes. Every time it goes off, I stop and get my coordinates from the GPS. I then transfer those to my paper map for practice.

3. I draw triangles, rectangles and squares on my map with a known starting point. I determine distance and headings for each turn. I then use only my compass and pace count beginning at the starting point and see how close I can get back to my exact starting point.

4. I use a pedometer on my boot to count steps. I will give myself a predetermined number of steps. Within those steps, I tell myself I must find ten edible foods. Every time I come to one, I mark it on my map using terrain association.

5. I get a map of the area and use my pace count to walk ridgelines or valleys to see what is most accurate. I will use my GPS as the judge to give me an accurate distance so I can check my pace count.

I bet you can think of one or two for yourself, can't you? You are limited only by your imagination. These sorts of activities makes wilderness navigation fun.

Here is a rundown on the different light sources I recommend for outdoor use:

- Headlamps are one of the most useful backcountry tools to come along in the past twenty years, in our opinion. A headlamp is easy to use and is an essential piece to keep both your hands free, so you can more effortlessly consult your compass or map.

- Tactical handheld flashlights offer various levels of brightness that will allow you to use only what you need. For example, the PowerTac E5 flashlight that we often carry has what is referred to as a "moonbeam" setting. When you are navigating at night and your eyes are used to the lack of light, the last thing you want is to throw out a beam of light that will temporarily blind you. A very low LED setting allows you to do that.

- Clip-on lights allow you to place a light nearly anywhere. I keep one clipped to either my shoulder strap or my Hill People Gear chest kit bag when I am outside after the sun sets.

- Colored lights or lenses offer advantages and disadvantages. Let's look briefly at each common color:

  - Red preserves your night vision and is hard to see at a distance, which assists your safety in a tactical situation. However, be aware that red light will often "wash out" any red lines on your map. Try it before you need it to see how well, or poorly, a red light affects your map reading.

  - Blue is also used to preserve night vision. Many people use blue lights to see blood at night. Blue also does a better job at cutting through foggy areas. That is why many car manufacturers make fog lights blue.

  - Green is used by many hunters and fisherman who suggest that it attracts rather than scares wildlife. Although we have not determined this to be true, it is quite possible.

- Snaplight glow sticks are "one and done" light sources, but they offer the wilderness navigator steady-on light. This advantage can save batteries, especially when you are navigating with partners.

MAP CASES

We mentioned these in chapter 1, but it is worthwhile to mention them again here. If you spend any amount of time in a wilderness, you are going to experience conditions in which your gear gets wet. Even daily dew will cause problems if your map is left out. A map case should be a part of your wilderness adventuring kit. At the very least, carry a plastic zip-top bag for this purpose. You can also cover your map with clear shipping tape. This allows you to draw on and fold the map easily as well.

ESTIMATING TIME FOR BACKCOUNTRY TRAVEL

William Naismith was a guy after our own hearts: He rather enjoyed a nice jaunt into the Scottish mountains in which he was born and lived. He came up with a formula, after much experience, that helps determine the time it takes to hike a mountainous or hilly area. The formula is beautiful in its simplicity and is loved by mountaineers all over the world for its accuracy. Naismith determined that the average person should allow 1 hour for every 3 miles (5 km) of travel. In addition to this, he determined you should add 30 minutes for every 1,000 feet (305 m) of ascent.

If, for example, I was going to make a 6-mile (10-km) hike that ascended 3,000 feet (915 m) in elevation, I could estimate that it would take me 2 hours + 1½ hours for a total of 3½ hours to make that entire hike.

Although Naismith did not calculate this into his formula, I have also done similar estimates based on descending a mountain or hill versus ascending. You would use the same 1 hour for every 3 miles (5 km) of travel, but you can take off 15 minutes for every 1,000 feet (305 km) of descent. This is on-trail ground that is easy to walk. On ground that is rough, Naismith's rule still applies. While it may seem like it would be easier to descend rough ground, it is actually just as hard as ascending it—just in a different way. Ground that is home to large boulders, ground that is uneven or ground that is loose is difficult to move across; therefore, it is going to be similar in timing to ascending.

CORDAGE

Cordage seems like such a simple thing, but it can be an excellent tool for determining distance on a map. You do not need the whole strand of it. Just one inner strand will be all you need. You can use any cordage that is thin but does not have much stretch to it. It is preferable if it does not have any stretch at all.

Very rarely does wilderness travel take you on a straight path from your starting point to your destination. You will notice that your scale on the bottom of your map is straight. But a piece of cordage allows you to get a good approximation measurement of a curvy trail or route. Lay your string on the map along a proposed route or known trail that you will be traveling on. "Pin" the string tightly to the starting and ending points on your map with your fingers. Then pick up the cordage, still gripping both ends, and transfer it to your scale. You may have to "choke up" on the string once a full scale has been measured, because your route may be longer than what your scale indicates. For instance, notice on the enclosed map that the scale at the bottom only covers 2 miles and 4 kilometers. If your route is longer than these distances, you will have to measure out a portion of the string then "choke up" on it to the new measuring point; that is, make multiple "end to end" measurements along the length of the string using the scale. Do this until you get a complete distance.

Please note that this is not an exact measurement. It is one more piece of the wilderness navigation puzzle to put in place for an accurate approximation of your position.

NOTEBOOK

A notebook should be a wilderness navigator's carryall container. It is our suggestion that you get one that borders on the "tactical" side (see image 46). These sorts of notebooks will have slots for pencils, a compass, notepaper and protractors as well as room for a small bag of Skittles thrown in for good measure. A good notebook also serves as a platform on which to put your map and utilize your map protractor while standing. I know that does not seem important, but it is one of the things that has come out of teaching our beginning students that helps tremendously. When you have a map, protractor, compass, pencil or strings in your hand and you're attempting to determine distances and headings, a sturdy notebook is very useful.

Using a notebook as a log checklist is another useful way you can use your notebook. You can use it during preplanning or while navigating:

- **Preplanning:** If you are planning a trip and are laying out expected routes, your notebook log will come in handy. You can list in order the notable points you will encounter. At each point you can list the distance and heading to the next point, so you don't need to utilize your map, compass or GPS along the way. You can obviously do this with your GPS as well. However, we still believe this sort of practice is a valuable training opportunity. It will enhance your ability to use the GPS receiver and understand it better.

Image 46: When you start, a good notebook will help you organize and utilize all your wilderness navigation tools.

- **Navigating:** You can collect points along your travel to verify with the map. This will serve as a method of quality assurance that you are traveling where you intend to and will give you a list of points and headings to follow if you want to go back the way you went in.

MARKERS AND SIGNS

When you start trekking and navigating the wilderness, you can add to your quality-control measures by using signs. Markers and signs in the wilderness come in many different forms. Many of those are placed by the entity that manages a wilderness (the US Forest Service, for example). Others are placed by users of the area. Many government-managed forests make it illegal to use your own markers, as they can cause confusion and serve to get others lost. With that said, you should be aware that markers are there and know what you are seeing. Let's discuss a few types of markers:

- **Signage:** Signs in the wilderness range from directional signs pointing to different features (see image 47) to distance signs telling the backcountry enthusiasts how far the next important feature is. Many of these are placed by the entity purposed with managing the area.

- **Paint:** Many public entities, divisions of forestry and private landowners use paint on trees to mark trails and boundary areas.

- **Metal or plastic badges:** Many of the national recreation trails now use badges that are nailed to trees. The nails are placed loosely so the tree can grow and the badge cannot be swallowed into the growth rings.

- **Ribbon:** Ribbon comes in many colors and is often used as a temporary marker. Foresters, biologists and surveyors use it regularly to mark areas they are surveying or studying. Since it is easy to use and carry, many hikers and hunters also utilize it to mark trails to stands or areas of interest. We recommend you not use ribbon for this purpose and instead use the other methods that we discussed in chapters 1 to 3 (such as a map, compass and GPS). If you must leave a trail, mark the ground with a scuff mark or form natural materials into an arrow to help guide your way. We also recommend that you not follow ribbon-marked trails. Ribbons can easily fall and a trail can then be easily lost.

- **Blazes:** Blazes are marks put on trees and used as trail markers. This is another form of signage that we don't recommend doing haphazardly, but is still regularly seen on many trails. When done properly, blazes do not negatively affect trees. If you are not familiar with this practice, you should also know that a small blaze cut onto a tree will often heal over in a season, requiring another tree to be cut. It is best to find alternative means to mark trails. Since blazes are easy for official personnel to use on government-owned land, you will see them used often.

- **Cairns and sticks (image 48):** Often, hikers and backpackers will utilize piles of rocks called cairns or a certain placement of sticks to provide a direction or marker. These markers can be as simple as a pile of rocks that help the user find the trail or an arrow made of sticks on the ground.

Image 47: Always use signage when available to provide quality control to where you think you are on the map.

Image 48: Rock cairns are sometimes used in the backcountry to help navigators keep on certain trails. They are often used at forks in roads and trails.

A UNIQUE BAG FOR WILDERNESS NAVIGATION

In my second book, *Ultimate Wilderness Gear*, I highlighted the Hill People Gear line of packs. One item I did not focus much attention on in that book is the Hill People Gear line of kit bags (see image 49).

These kit bags serve many purposes, but we feel they are an excellent choice for wilderness navigation. Depending on which bag you get, you will get main pockets that include small pockets and dividers as well as attachment points within them. Some of the bags have Pouch Attachment Ladders System (PALS) webbing on them for attaching specific items. For example, I have webbing pouches for my radio, weapon magazines and water bottles. If you have a gear piece that you need to have quick or regular access to, most likely there is a pouch made for it.

My Hill People Gear Original kit bag is my go-to wilderness navigation carrier. It is comfortable, can carry essential safety and survival supplies and—as this chapter's title hints at—you can look cool while carrying it.

Image 49: The Hill People Gear kit bag is a great way to carry essential tools close to you.

TROUBLESHOOTING: OVERCOMING COMMON PROBLEMS WITH GEAR

There are a lot of extra items in this chapter to consider when it comes to troubleshooting. I have covered most of them throughout the text, but there are a few that should be covered here as well, especially as we start putting all of these together. Consider the following as you purchase and use navigation gear:

- Pace count beads can be purchased or made yourself. I recommend making them yourself. I have noticed, after teaching many students, that homemade pace count beads actually get used more often. It is a little thing, but it may be the difference between your actually using your pace count (which can be vital to your safety) and not using it.

- Light sources are key to using your map in low- or no-light situations. A bright tactical light has a "washout" effect, which effectively makes you blind in the dark once the light is turned off. Always use the lowest setting possible in those conditions. Even better is using a colored lens to get that work done in the dark. Colored lenses have a negligible effect on your eyesight when they are turned off and you return to darkened conditions. When possible, it is best to take a few moments to let your eyes adjust to the dark when you have been looking at a map using a light.

- When using a protractor on your map, it is sometimes difficult to find grid lines or the edge of the map that match for accuracy. You may need to add your own lines to the map to facilitate this. Remember that many software and online programs can do this rather easily by just adjusting the settings.

QUESTIONS FOR PRACTICE

1. When choosing a grid tool to work with your map, what is a very important aspect you should be aware of before purchasing?

2. Knowing how many steps you take for a given distance is known as what?

3. Knowing how much time it takes you to travel a given distance is known as what?

4. The device that can quickly tell you your distance above sea level is known as what?

5. True or false: Using a 1:24000 protractor on a 1:12000 map is close enough for wilderness navigation.

6. What scale of protractor will you need to work with the map that is provided you in this book?

7. What is your pace count?

8. What is the best color of light source to use when doing wilderness navigation?

9. Name one inexpensive way to waterproof your map for use in the field.

10. Name one good reason why a high-quality notebook is an important piece of navigation equipment.

Answers: (1) The scales need to match on both. (2) Pace count. (3) Time count. (4) Altimeter. (5) False. (6) 1:24000. (7) This is different for all readers, but you should take time to ascertain your pace count now so you have it when you need it. (8) White. However, use another color, such as red, if you are using it for tactical purposes. (9) Place it in a zip-top storage bag; cover it in clear shipping tape. (10) It serves as a platform for your map; it keeps multiple related items together.

GET OUT AND PRACTICE

The components we've gone over in this chapter have added in a well-rounded use of the gear and equipment that you can use to nearly complete the wilderness navigation puzzle we keep talking about. Most of these items here are those that enhance modern wilderness navigation experiences. The more you carry, the more accurate and efficient you become. In a practice where you carry everything on your back, this can be burdensome. This is why you need to get out and practice your skills to see what things you feel are necessary to your abilities as a wilderness navigator.

We have several short trips that will take you through all the details needed. Following are the condensed instructions for going on any trip:

Always engage in thorough preplanning:

❑ Tell someone where you are going and what time you expect to be out of the wilderness.

❑ Leave the contact number of the emergency responders for the area you will be traveling in.

❑ Leave a description of the clothing you are wearing, gear items you are carrying and shoes you are wearing.

When it comes time to pack for your trip, remember the following:

❑ Take a wilderness navigation kit, which includes at a minimum a baseplate compass, topography map of the area, pace count beads, notebook, pencil and straightedge.

❑ Add other items, such as a GPS, altimeter and radio for an enhanced (and perhaps safer) experience.

❑ Remember your survival kit (see page 150).

(continued)

☐ Start your hike completely hydrated. This helps your mental attitude as well as your bodily needs. Take a minimum of 32 ounces (960 ml) of water with you. The amount of water you take will depend greatly on your size and health and the weather conditions.

Remember to do the following during your after-trip review:

☐ Write some notes about your experience. These should include who went with you, what you did for wilderness navigation practice and when you did it (include the time of day and year) and where you traveled. The last portion should detail approximately how many miles you covered, where it was and other pertinent details.

☐ Place your navigation kit in a location where the compass will not be exposed to extreme heat or cold (this causes issues for the fluid in the bezel). Do not store your compass in direct contact with other magnetized or metallic items.

☐ Clean your gear and put it away.

At this point, we are going to offer several different practical exercises because we have covered so much! For some of these exercises, we will ask you to use the enclosed map; for others, you will use your imagination.

Image 50: Continuing education and practice is a must-do item of developing a good wilderness navigation skill set.

OTHER ITEMS YOU NEED TO DO LAND NAVIGATION
RIGHT OR TO LOOK COOL (OR BOTH)

PRACTICAL EXERCISE 1:
DETERMINING AN ACCURATE BEARING

There are two ways to get a highly accurate bearing from one location to another. You will use the enclosed map to assist you in doing this. (As a refresher, a bearing is one of the directions from 0 degrees to 360 degrees. You should always measure the number clockwise from due north, which is 360 degrees.)

You are going to determine your bearing in six steps. Steps 1 and 6 are ways of developing quick visual quality-assurance estimates. Steps 2, 3, 4 and 5 are ways to get very accurate readings. For this exercise, let's assume that you are camping at the Twin Knobs campground (found on the northeastern side of your map). You have a reliable canoe and a fishing partner to go with you. You have heard that there is some good fishing where Caney Creek and Sulphur Branch flow into Cave Run Lake. You want to head that direction but also want to practice your navigation skills along the way. Assume you are putting your canoe in at the westernmost point of the Twin Knobs campground area and paddling across the lake to the location. Follow these steps:

1. Determine just by looking at the map a general sense of direction and at least one feature along the way that can help you verify you are going the right direction. Leaving the campground will be a relatively straight paddle due west, 270 degrees map. Don't forget that you have two-degree measurements used regularly: your map reading, which you obtain by using only your map (in this case referred to as 270 degrees map); and degrees magnetic, which is what you use on your compass (this would be your reading after adjusting for declination). This is covered in the sidebar entitled "Deciphering Declination" (page 32). The scale tells you the trip is a little over 2 miles (3.5 km) one way. About 2 miles (3.5 km) into the paddle, you should see a small cove that is an estimated 200 degrees map of your canoe position in the center of the large cove. You will use these estimations to later give quality assurance to the ones you determine with other equipment.

2. Use a protractor to determine the bearing from the campground to the fishing spot as well as the angle from that direct line to the cove that will be on your left, or south, along the tip. To do this, draw a straight line from the tip of the campground directly to the fishing spot. Then draw another line that starts at that line and bisects the small southside cove. Then use the protractor as we did earlier in this chapter to determine these bearings (see page 106). You should come up with 272 degrees map from the campground to the fishing spot and 209 degrees map for the small cove to the south.

3. Use your baseplate compass to determine the angles. You can use the same lines drawn in step 2. Lay the side of your baseplate compass along the first line. Align the orienting lines within the bezel to the grid lines on the map and make them parallel.

4. Pick up your compass and read the number on the same line as the direction of travel line on your compass. You should get 271 degrees and 209 degrees for the two lines.

5. Use your GPS or Gaia app to set three waypoints (for a refresher on particular apps, see page 76). Set a waypoint on the western side of the campground, one at the fishing spot and another at the end of the small cove. The one at the end of the small cove should be on the imaginary line that bisects the middle of the cove. You should finally set a waypoint where the primary travel line intersects the line that bisects the small cove. Utilize your preferred device to travel from each of the waypoints to the others. When you tell the device to go from one waypoint to another, it will give you a compass reading (verify in your settings whether this is a map or magnetic reading). Note that I used both my Garmin Foretrex 401 and the Gaia app for this exercise. For the primary travel line, I got 271.3 degrees map and 208.8 degrees for the small cove.

6. Repeat step 1. Doing this makes sure that the readings you got on your equipment matches up to what you visually see on your map. As the troubleshooting sections indicate, there are a few things that can go wrong when using any of these methods, and it is wise to double-check.

PRACTICAL EXERCISE 2:
GOING ON AND OFF THE TRAIL TO DEVELOP SKILLS

For this exercise, assume that you want to go out and practice the newfound skills you have picked up in this book or a wilderness navigation class like we teach at Nature Reliance School. You recognize that you are new to this practice. Therefore, you are going to stay on a trail and walk less than 5 miles (8 km) on it. Consider you are going to do this on the hike depicted in image 51.

Utilizing the road next to Clear Creek Lake, use a GPS to get a length of 330 feet (100 m). Utilize this distance to get your pace count (see page 108). Determine the distance you will walk on the trail from starting point A to ending point B, then answer the following questions:

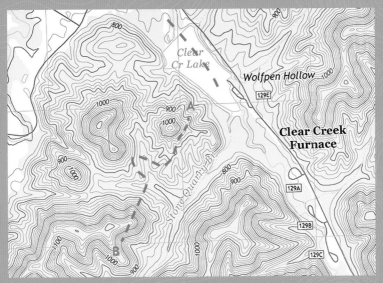

Image 51: Finding an area you are familiar with will allow you to start practicing wilderness navigation skills.

1. What is the elevation at starting point A?

2. Stopping at the midway point of the hike, what features will you find to the north, south, east and west of where you are standing once you get there?

3. Take an azimuth from the ending position to the center of Clear Creek Lake. If you were to walk directly to that lake from your ending point, what would the degrees magnetic be? Remember to figure in your declination.

4. Is this short trail walk going to be in a forested area or in an open field?

Now that we have accomplished those tasks, let's have some more fun with wilderness navigation in the same areas. Note in image 51 the path you will need to take to navigate around Clear Creek Lake. To navigate around the lake, you will take your initial azimuth and then turn the four 90-degree turns that are depicted. You can do this by one of two methods:

1. Walk the angles and add or subtract the 90 degrees on your compass each time you need to make a turn. You will also need to utilize your pace count around the obstacle. Measure and determine what the approximate distance is for each section to avoid this obstacle. Convert that number to your pace count. In this manner, you do not have to do math in your head as you walk—you simply walk the determined number of paces.

Answers: (1) 880 feet (268 m). (2) North, a hillside; south, an open field, slowly ascending hill and creek; east, the general direction you came from; west, a short ravine leading to another ridgeline. (3) 29 degrees magnetic. (4) Forested area.

Image 52: Some navigators will hold the side of the compass and keep the direction of travel static when negotiating around obstacles.

2. Utilizing your pace count is the same for this method, but you will utilize your compass differently. Instead of changing your compass at each turn, keep your compass on the same azimuth reading the entire trip around the obstacle. Since these are short distances of 330 feet (100 m) or less, you can do this and simply hold the compass turned sideways (image 52) so that the direction-of-travel arrow is pointing in the same direction. Some people find this more confusing, others find it less confusing. Find the method that suits your needs best.

PRACTICAL EXERCISE 3:
GOING ON AN OVERNIGHT HIKE

Going on a two-day, one-night hike is not difficult under any circumstances. It is our hope that the wheels are already turning on what you would need to do and carry for such a trip. If you go through the three steps listed at the beginning of this "Get Out and Practice" section, you will note that the trip is the same as exercise 1, except you will need to take a few other items to make you more comfortable:

1. You will need some food to eat in the backcountry.

2. You will need either a hammock, tent or tarp setup and other creature comforts to make your overnight stay comfortable. (For an in-depth analysis on gear, including food and sleep gear, pick up my book *Ultimate Wilderness Gear*.)

When it comes to wilderness navigation, you will be using the same equipment listed at the beginning of this chapter (page 104). If you are in the high mountains, an altimeter will also serve you well. An overnight stay does add difficulty. Your wilderness navigation skills will help overcome those difficulties. Specifically, unless you want to carry all your water, you will want to analyze the map to see where you can gather and filter or purify water along the way. It is also in your best interest to preplan a place that you might like to have as a camping spot. Preplan for these things by consulting your map.

Consider the following image (image 53a), which you'll notice is a portion of the map enclosed in this book. A good friend or family member is going to drop you off at the spot marked on the map. As you consult the map, you see that you have three different directions and three spots to set up a camp, stay the night and hike back out to the same spot you were dropped off at. Let's assume you want to stay on a trail and not deviate from it. If we assume that you are new to hiking and 5 miles (8 km) is a good range for a beginner to hike in a day, we have picked three different possible campsites for you that are marked as A, B and C. Here are some questions to help you analyze this situation:

1. Which trip and campsite offers you the best opportunity to find water? (Keep in mind you will need to filter or purify it.)

2. Put together a log for each trip that notes the distances, elevation and headings. Looking at each log, which trip seems to be the easiest walking? The hardest?

Here are some things of definite consideration for each of these trips:

1. Trip A starts out relatively flat, has one hill to climb, crosses the highway and drops back down into a much larger hollow. There is a fair amount of off-trail travel, which would require you to regularly utilize terrain association or use GPS to pinpoint your location. There are ample opportunities to find water at the beginning but the other streams may not hold water year-round, as evidenced by the portions that are dotted. If water becomes an issue on trip A, you can always travel to the lake to get some near the campsite.

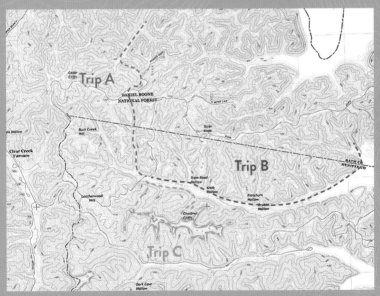

Image 53a: Three different hikes in the same area will offer you different choices and considerations for an overnight trip.

2. Trip B is an incredibly easy hike going downhill, and terrain association could be used to navigate this entire route with or without a compass. Simply by counting the hollows and ravines to the north of the route, you could keep up with your position and find your way into the McIntosh Branch hollow to find an isolated campsite near the lake.

3. Trip C is the most difficult and dangerous of the trips, and it is an exploratory hike that takes you up one of the only access points to the top of Chestnut Cliffs. The walk explores each small finger leading out to the cliff line, allowing you to discover and get good vistas of the hilltop and all the surrounding areas. It leads down another steep slope, but the descent does not require ropes. If water is needed on this trip, you will have no access to any except at the beginning and the very end of the trip. Take plenty with you.

Considering that there are a broad range of readers for this text, there can be no definitive answer as to which of the preceding trips is best. One person may be young and able to carry all their water with them. Another will not want to carry any water if they do not have to and will want to stop often. Some see hiking as a way to challenge themselves physically and will want to go up in elevation as much as possible. Others may want to take a more leisurely path to their campsite. Whatever your choice is, we want you to see how important it is to make a log or maybe even a profile map (image 53b) of your trip.

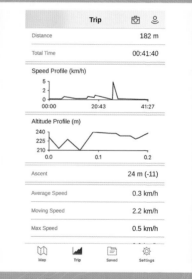

Image 53b: This profile diagram was taken from a Gaia iOS app. It lets you know the elevation changes on a proposed trip.

PRACTICAL EXERCISE 4:
GOING ON A MULTIDAY HIKE

It is now time for you to get out and practice a multiday hike.

Going on a multiday backpacking trip can be an incredibly rewarding experience for many reasons. It can also be a major pain in the back (literally!) if it does not go well. Adequate map and compass skills can assist you in making your trip safer and one that meets the skill level of those going on the trip. The last thing you want to do is set out on what is supposed to be an easy hiking trip and be surprised by ascending several hundred feet in elevation right at the start.

Preplanning a trip is just as important as getting a pack. Utilizing a map for preplanning is critical—especially for an excursion in which you will be away from quick and easy rescue. For most multiday backpacking trips, isolation is a given. Most people want to hike to get away from others and to go deep into a wilderness. I am much the same way and like to get out and away when I can. I also like to make sure I plan accordingly so I am safe and my needs (such as water) are taken care of.

Here are some important steps to consider when finding a location during a multiday trip:

1. Follow all the gear recommendations you have read in this book. The biggest morale killer for outdoor fun is not sleeping and eating well. You will need to bring adequate gear for your sleeping and eating needs. If you need help with that, pick up my book *Ultimate Wilderness Gear*. In it, I have whole chapters dedicated to both of those morale busters and discuss ways to overcome them.

2. Know your physical capabilities. I recommend 5 to 10 miles (8 to 16 km) per day for individuals new to hiking and backpacking. Many can cover a lot more than that. By only planning on 5 to 10 miles (8 to 16 km), you are supplied with plenty of time and terrain along the way to practice wilderness navigation skills. You most likely did not ride your bike on the first try. You are also not going to get wilderness navigation skills on the first try either. The more you practice, the more competent you will become.

3. Don't overlook anything during preplanning. Here are some vital areas of importance related to navigation that you should note during your preplanning:

   1. Elevation changes: You must look at these so you know what to expect. Will you be going uphill, going downhill or traversing flat ground most of the day?

   2. Water sources: You will want to start hydrated, as well as carry some water with you. How much you carry will depend on how many sources of water there are in the area. For instance, ridgelines rarely offer water while ravines often do.

   3. Camping locations: Depending on your location, there may only be certain approved areas to camp. You should know this before starting. You don't want to find that you have 23 miles (37 km) to the next camping spot at 2:00 p.m. Use your scale to calculate the distances between those locations.

   4. Risks along the way: You should know where there are cliff lines and other such features. If not, you may leave the trail to go to the bathroom and find yourself slipping off a cliff.

   5. Pickup and drop-off: You may be hiking with a friend or family member and have vehicles on both ends of the hike. If not, you should study your hike so you can communicate the pickup time and location with someone else. Whenever possible, don't keep your pickup friend waiting on you for extended periods of time. You want them to stay happy so they will shuttle you again in the future.

   6. After-action review (AAR): Immediately after you get home safely and get cleaned up, do an AAR of the trip. Write some notes on the various legs of the trip. What went well and what went poorly? Keep this AAR in a place where you can easily find it and read it again before your next trip—it should always be part of your preplanning.

PRACTICAL EXERCISE 5:
TRAVELING BY CANOE OR KAYAK

I will never forget my first use of wilderness navigation in stressful conditions. It was a situation in which doing some preplanning with a map and some basic natural navigation allowed a friend and me to do a self-rescue.

In Kentucky, we are fond of saying, "If you don't like the weather, wait a few minutes." This was certainly true for a friend and me on a canoe trip in the spring of 1996. There had been heavy spring rains, and the rivers and creeks were swollen with water. This ensured that two young, experienced paddlers were ready to go out and enjoy the rapids. Despite our eagerness to get on the water, we did take a look at a USGS topo map of the area. We had been on enough trips that, despite our excellent success rate, we realized sometimes unexpected things happen and you need to get assistance or walk out on your own for self-rescue. This was long before cell phones were a common thing for individuals to carry. We had no GPS, so we memorized notable points along the route and made mental checks for those points along the paddle.

We noted that there was a distinct point of change for our rescue plans. Self-rescue is simply the act of handling a disaster on your own and making your way out. Rather than sit on the side of the river and wait possibly twenty-four hours or more for a search-and-rescue team, we determined to hike out ourselves. As we approached an area known as the Narrows, there was a very distinct turn in the river that headed southward. The turn in the river was near 90 degrees, and we simply could not miss it. We determined prior to that point that if we needed to self-rescue, we would exit on the west side of the river because there was a road within walking distance. We also determined that if something happened to us at this noteworthy point or beyond, we would exit the river to the east. On that side, there was a well-known trail that would take us to where our vehicle was parked.

Our preplanning saved our lives that day. Wild rivers are powerful forces of nature, and the Rockcastle River proved this to us. In one swift movement coming out of an eddy, our canoe got hung on a rock and folded in half. After throwing us out of it, it eventually became free but got stuck downstream on a rock in the middle of the river. After many attempts, we were unable to free it from the rapids. We were forced to leave due to the cold weather and the fear of hypothermia.

With only the clothes on our backs, we made our way east out of the river to the trail and then hiked to our vehicle. This is where we recognized another issue: We had our shuttle driver, who had taken my truck to the drop-off point, place my key under the floor mat and lock up the truck. I had an extra set of keys that were with me in the canoe, which was now stuck in the middle of the river. We tried many different ways to break into my own vehicle to get the keys. Eventually, I made the hard decision to shatter one of the windows. Getting in the vehicle to dry clothes and a heater was essential to our survival at that point. We covered up the window and headed back home. We came back the next day to gather up what gear we could, counted ourselves fortunate and chalked up the experience to wilderness education.

Wilderness navigation can save lives. My friend and I are here to prove it.

You can consider a river or stream much like a long trail. The use of wilderness navigation is not all that different. The main difference is the need to have waterproof gear for both your comfort and for any land navigation needs you might have. Let me emphasize a couple of interesting points here:

1. My friend and I used the sun and natural navigation to determine an approximate direction for east and west (you'll learn about this in chapter 6).

2. My friend and I made a logbook in our minds of different parts of the river we would be encountering.

Let's assume that you want to go on a paddling excursion and you want to do it safely. Remember to do the following to keep yourself and others safe:

1. Have your situational awareness turned on at all times when paddling. Constantly monitor what is ahead of you with your eyes and ears. If you hear rushing water, or you see that the shore or tree line ahead of you seems to drop off, then you need to get to the shore and check out what is going on. You may be headed over a steep drop-off unexpectedly. This goes for all waterways. Each waterway has its own behavior and character in different seasons, as well as water levels.

2. Take a waterproof GPS and keep it on your life vest on the trip. You could set it during preplanning to offer audible alarms for possible dangerous points along the way. This would allow you to adjust accordingly as you're paddling. I want to emphasize that having a GPS does not replace using situational awareness and paying attention to your surroundings. Nothing could be further from the truth. I believe that a human's cognitive ability for problem solving and situational awareness is incredible. A GPS should add to your ability to be proactive about dangerous situations.

3. Note all possible dangerous locations on your map during preplanning. You should also recognize that due to the flow of debris in water, obstacles could be in places you would never expect them.

4. Whenever possible, contact locals or guides in the area when you plan on traveling a waterway. Locals especially will have intimate knowledge of the waterway and how it is flowing. This is beneficial in two directions: If the water is flowing really hard, the paddle may be more dangerous. If the water is flowing very gently or not at all, you may be in for a very long drag of your canoe rather than a paddle.

5. Backups are essential for wilderness navigation and, in my estimation, more so on a paddling trip. Bring a waterproof map case, along with a baseplate compass. There are so many things that can go wrong with a GPS around water (including heavy rain) that you should have these backups.

6. During risk analysis of the trip, you should plan for extract should someone need medical attention for any reason. Moving water—even slow-moving water—can be dangerous. The quickest way out may be downstream, or it may be cross-country from your location at the time of need. This is not something you want plan for in the middle of the event. Preplan this contingency before going by terrain analysis.

CHAPTER 5

WHAT TO DO IF IT ALL GOES WRONG

You can't climb up a mountain with downhill thoughts.
—Anonymous

"That others may live" is the motto of US Air Force Special Operations Pararescue teams. Some form or another of that motto has been put forward by first responders, including civilian search-and-rescue teams, for many years. It is uncommon for gear belonging to one lost hiker to be utilized to provide the same safety net for two other lost hikers, but that is exactly what happened with the gear that belonged to John Donovan.

Donovan went missing on May 2, 2005, while hiking on the Pacific Crest Trail. During the time he was lost, Donovan kept a journal on the back of some maps and sketch paper that he carried in his pack. In his last journal entry, Donovan indicated that he was without hope of ever being found.

What is profoundly odd is that two hikers, Brandon Day and Gina Allen, stumbled across Donovan's lost gear after they themselves had become lost in the San Jacinto Wilderness. Day and Allen had been on a short tourist excursion when they wandered away from their group, became disoriented and wound up completely lost with only the clothes they had on them. After they spent a cold desert night in a cave, they followed a stream through some difficult terrain.

The pair came across the abandoned campsite and gear that had belonged to Donovan. A closer inspection of the gear led them to conclude that the gear had been abandoned for quite some time. It was then that they discovered Donovan's journal entries. The last one was dated exactly one year to the day of their finding it. They were able to find some better clothing and matches in the gear that they later used to start a signal fire. The signal fire led rescuers to see their position.

Despite Donovan's disappearance, he was able, through the gear that he had brought with him, to help save the lives of the two lost hikers.

It may seem obvious, but it is worth driving home that the best way to survive an outdoor trip is to take precautions to avoid dangerous situations in the first place. But if we don't know how or why we get lost, it's hard to know how to circumvent it. This conundrum leads us to an important question.

WHY DO WE GET LOST?

There are many reasons we get lost, all of which have one underlying theme: lack of situational awareness. We discussed that in chapter 4. What we did not discuss in that chapter is how a lack of situational awareness increases our chances of getting lost. The following sections are a few reasons that you might lose your way. Learn to resist these, and you will dramatically decrease your chances of needing recovery.

WALKING IN CIRCLES

There are two reasons we tend to walk in circles. The first is that we are left- or right-foot dominant just as we are left- or right-hand dominant. This supports the notion that when we walk toward an obstruction, we tend to drift by pushing off with our dominant foot. Second, there are very few of us that have perfect symmetry when it comes to leg length. Most of us have one leg that is longer than the other. This causes a shorter stride length on one side. Both of these factors contribute to a drift that on the personal level is nearly imperceptible. On a larger scale, it is much more noticeable. This means you and I will not notice it in our own steps, but if we had the vantage point of being overhead in an open area it would be easy to see the drift that leads to walking in circles.

Walking in circles is rather simple to prevent: Alternate which side you travel on when you come to obstructions. So, if you come to a large sinkhole and travel left to navigate around it, navigate right when you come to a thick growth of rhododendron. Whatever the obstructions might be, simply keep track of your travel and alternate each time.

HAVING NORMALCY BIAS

We humans do not like change. We are naturally predisposed to want things to be normal. Therefore, when things are (or even seem) out of place, we will do things in our mind to make them normal. In wilderness navigation, this means that if we are unknowingly in the process of getting lost, our minds will normalize it. For example, we may have taken a wrong trail and recognize that it does not look familiar. We will tell ourselves that things have changed, and we won't remember similar things to normalize the situation. We keep walking farther and getting even more lost.

To combat normalcy bias, you have to let go of your ego and stay in control of your own emotions. When you recognize that you do not know where you are, you *must* stop. Start using all your wilderness navigation skills to scientifically break things down—in other words, look at the situation from a calm, cool and cognitive perspective rather than an emotional one.

EXPERIENCING FOCUS LOCK

The best example of focus lock in the modern world is people walking into things while they are looking at their cell phones. They are locked on the phone and not aware of what is going on around them. On the trail, we can get focused on many things. Pain due to an injury, the offensive smell we are putting off or a beautiful vista in front of us. Any of these can rob us of our focus. When we are focused on those types of things, we cannot be totally aware of what is going on around us.

If you have followed Nature Reliance School much at all, it is not hard to notice that we love tracking. Trackers are some of the guiltiest people in the world at getting focus locked on the ground in front of them. Trackers and you can combat focus lock in two different ways:

- **Look up and out and often.** Simple, yes, but profoundly important to having good situational awareness in the outdoors. I take the time to look up and out at regular intervals to see what is going on. You can add this to your growing wilderness navigation skill set. On a regular basis and for no apparent reason other than practice, get out your map and compass and take a reading or two so you can see up and out in front of you.

- **Ask yourself regularly, "What am I missing?"** Our minds will wander and get in a rut on a hike. When this happens, it is easy to miss all the things that we came to the wilderness to experience. When I recognize my mind is wandering to work or other issues, I stop my thoughts, look around and focus some attention on what I am hearing in an effort to notice what I am missing. This one tidbit will enhance your outdoor experiences, I can promise you that.

145

NOT MONITORING THE BASELINE

Baseline is the way in which an environment (the whole area or a portion of it) appears in its most natural state. Disturbance is anything that causes disruption to the baseline. If we do not monitor the areas we are adventuring in—and why wouldn't we, since it is the whole reason we went outside?—we miss the subtle cues that help us stay safe. Working terrain association is a good example of this. If you are following a contour level around a mountain and come to an obstacle, you will have the choice to go up or down to avoid the obstacle. If you don't monitor the baseline, you could easily begin to drift downhill and wind up significantly off your original contour.

To effectively monitor your baseline, you will need to spend more time outside. (You are welcome that I have given you permission to do so.) In all seriousness, spending more time outside gives you the experience to understand what the baseline is. As an example, my family was recently told there was an area that contained wild blueberries in the national forest. In Kentucky, there are a lot of wild blackberries and raspberries, but blueberries don't appear often. It is legal and acceptable to harvest them in this area. So I traveled to the area and used my Gaia phone app to find the highest point near where we were told the blueberries were. I could then look around to find an area that looked like it had experienced forest fire in the past five years. Blueberries like to grow in these former burn sites. By seeing the baseline of the areas from above, it was easy to determine where the burn site was then navigate to it using the Gaia app. Once there, we were able to harvest a couple gallons of blueberries and leave many more for other visitors and the wildlife.

RELYING ON CONFUSED MENTAL MAPS

Relying on confused mental maps is similar to harboring normalcy bias but is more specific to wilderness navigation. You will see in the following section that preplanning is vital to your safety during wilderness navigation. We can collect information from outside influences, such as maps and people, before heading into an environment. The area may be one we are new to, or it may be one we are familiar with but our previous experience there was a long time ago. It is the thoughts the outside influences give us and the old memories that can be the beginning of a confused mental map. Consider that you are going on a canoe trip and one of your friends, who has paddled the river, tells you there is a class III rapid directly after the three creeks that flow into the river on the east side. Once you pass those three creeks, you don't see any rapids at all. This is because your mental map of the area was compromised by your friend who was an outside influence.

To combat forming a confused mental map, there is an old bird-watcher's adage that I keep in mind: "When the bird and the bird book disagree, always believe the bird." We can get focused on what we think, maybe even what we have been educated on, and think it must be that way always. Nature is ever changing—we must open our eyes and pay attention to what we are seeing, even if that disagrees with our preconceived thoughts or education on the issue.

BEING COCKY (INSTEAD OF CONFIDENT)

To do something in a wilderness environment—such as climb several hundred vertical feet, rappel off a 300-foot (91-m) cliff line, paddle a raging river or hike into an area known for grizzly bears—you should have a strong mind-set. Cockiness leads wilderness adventurers to have poor decision-making skills and to ignore necessary safety protocols. Confidence is the mind-set that we recommend adventure travelers develop. Confidence is based in education and experience, not in false bravado. We bring this up because some of the search-and-rescue efforts that have occurred across the country have turned into body recoveries because of cockiness on the part of the victim. There is nothing wrong with engaging in dangerous activities (you can be assured that we do so); however, we participate in them after much training and risk assessment and analysis. By considering the risks and answers to possible issues, we can more safely enjoy those dangerous activities that could possibly get us lost or injured in the backcountry.

WHEN THE UNEXPECTED HAPPENS

The preceding sections name some common reasons you may find yourself lost. It is valuable to understand this so you can recognize when you are doing them during wilderness navigation. But sometimes stuff happens. It could be an injury, a mislabeled map or a sprung compass. Whatever the case may be, things happen on occasion that make utilizing your wilderness navigation skills ineffective. Since the unexpected can happen to the best of us, it is necessary that we cover what to do when you are lost and need assistance. This is where search-and-rescue teams get to work. What I will do in a situation such as this is make it easier for SAR to find me. We need to cover rescue in three distinct processes: preplanning, determining the viability of self-rescue and communicating for rescue.

PREPLANNING

Let's first consider a checklist of items and things to do while you are preplanning your wilderness navigation needs. Each of the following should be considered before you go outdoors:

- **Inspect your compass.** Get it out before your trip and verify that there are no bubbles in the housing and that it points north properly.

- **Verify that you have the map of the area in which you want to travel.** Utilize some sort of map case to protect the map from moisture and wilderness conditions. The last thing you want is for your map to get snagged on a briar and rip, rendering an important section of the map unreadable.

- **Use your map to analyze your trail.** This will give you valuable preplanning opportunities to find water and campsites and better understand the terrain you will be walking. Preplanning in this way will help you develop the right mind-set for the work ahead.

- **Check that your GPS has full battery power as you start your trip.** Also verify that you have backup batteries. Use a meter to ensure your backup batteries are fully charged as well.

- **Phone a friend or family member.** One of the most important things you can do is tell someone where you are going, who you are going with and when you expect to return. There are too many stories of people experiencing tragedy in the wilderness due to not completing this one small task. (For some of those stories and for more ways to solve these issues, read my first book, *Extreme Wilderness Survival*.) Make sure that the person you contact is trustworthy and will contact authorities if you do not show up at the designated place or time. It will be even more helpful if you leave the following information with your contact:

  - Medical and allergy needs.

  - Make, model and license plate number of your vehicle.

  - Map with approximate plans.

  - Phone numbers for emergency personnel should you not return.

  - Radio (bonus for you if you know the frequency that the area SAR communicate on, or if you have a radio that can search for frequencies).

- Names and phone numbers of those in your hiking party (SAR teams will frequently call these numbers to attempt contact).

Wilderness survival, in my opinion, is mostly a game of preplanning. With that in mind, check out the sidebar "Basic Seventy-Two-Hour Survival Kit for Wilderness Travel" (page 150) for a quick list of survival items you should always take with you whether you are going out for an hour or a week.

DETERMINING THE VIABILITY OF SELF-RESCUE

When are you lost?

This question is more difficult to answer than you might think. Basically, as soon as you don't know where you are, you are lost. But that does not mean it is time to sit down and await rescue.

There are many times I don't know where I am when outdoors; however, that does *not* mean I don't have some sort of system to both locate myself and get home safely. Let's consider an example. Earlier we discussed catching features (page 65). You may recall that a catching feature comes into play when you set an azimuth and travel along it until you come to the catching feature, which may be something like a river, road or mountain range. Once there, you use your compass and terrain association to home in on your actual destination. Along that entire trip, you most likely don't know where you are, but you are not lost.

In my first book, *Extreme Wilderness Survival*, I shared a concept that is vitally important to understanding when you are lost. I refer to it as the Critical Rule of Three. This rule states that if three anomalies exist in a given wilderness situation, you must at that point change what you are doing. In wilderness navigation, we can apply the Critical Rule of Three like this: You are unsure of your whereabouts, and you get out your map and compass. You take a bearing along the land feature you are currently on and recognize that the area of the map you thought you were on does not match up to the degree reading you just got. That is anomaly number one. You immediately stop and find other land features to take readings on and see if they match up to where you are. If you have a GPS, you should also get it out and pinpoint your location. Find that location on the map. If at any point during this process you have two or more anomalies that simply do not match up, then you must stop. Put everything away for a moment and do what you can to clear your head. Drink some water to get hydrated. After taking a short break, it's time to determine if you should stay put or self-rescue.

BASIC SEVENTY-TWO-HOUR SURVIVAL KIT FOR WILDERNESS TRAVEL

You should carry the following supplies into the wilderness each time you go (bear in mind these items are the minimum you should carry). All of these items will weigh less than 2 pounds (900 g) when assembled and can easily be carried in a small over-the-shoulder bag, fanny pack, backpack or even large cargo pockets of your pants:

1. Wilderness navigation supplies: a topography map, compass, GPS (if desired), notebook and pencil, straightedge and backup batteries for all electronics (including your light source) will help you navigate accurately.

2. First aid kit: Boo-boo supplies as well as trauma items. Boo-boo items are those that you use regularly such as adhesive bandages, small gauze squares, moleskin and over-the-counter medicines. Trauma items would include hemostatic gauze, a tourniquet, nasopharyngeal airway and similar items. (Be sure you undertake proper training to use the trauma items.)

3. Whistle: A whistle is a good thing for all adventurers to carry, and it is a must-have for all children.

4. Brightly colored bandana: A bandana can be employed for various purposes but especially for signaling—fluorescent yellow or orange are good choices.

5. Shelter: At a minimum, pack a 55-gallon (208-L) garbage bag if you are traveling light, or a 9 x 9-foot (2.75 x 2.75-m) tarp if carrying more is a possibility.

6. Firestarting equipment: This includes a lighter, a ferrocerium rod and some SOLKOA Fastfire™ brand tinder cubes.

7. Water purification equipment: Take a stainless steel water bottle so you can boil water, and also include a purifying straw (such as a Rapid Pure).

8. Artificial light source: A good headlamp is a great choice.

SURVIVAL FUNDAMENTALS

If you want to pursue in-depth survival study, then please pick up my book *Extreme Wilderness Survival* if you haven't yet. Even without that resource, however, you should have a fundamental understanding of how to handle yourself in any survival situation. At Nature Reliance School, our focus is on mind-set, skills, tactics and gear (in that order). To have a proper mind-set, you should understand the following concepts for all survival events.

The acronym STOPA helps you remember what to do under stress. Let's break the acronym down:

1. Stop: Literally stop what you are doing and sit down. This serves to calm you and keeps you from getting even more lost or injured.
2. Think: Think about what you have with you that can be used to signal for help or keep you alive.
3. Observe: Observe your surroundings to see what you can use to protect yourself from the elements.
4. Plan: Make a plan for how you will stay alive (discuss it with others if you are in a group).
5. Act: Keep your mind active, do not give up, stay alive!

The Critical Rule of Three is a way to prioritize your survival needs. It helps you remember that even though your stomach may be growling, you need to concern yourself with other priorities first. This is a general understanding of your needs, and these times are not absolutes. Nevertheless, the Critical Rule of Three is worth memorizing:

1. Three minutes for air and blood: You cannot live more than three minutes without oxygen and blood flow continuing in your body.
2. Three hours for core body temperature: You cannot live more than three hours without maintaining your core body temperature.
3. Three days for hydration: You cannot live more than three days without maintaining or obtaining hydration for your body.
4. Three weeks for food: You cannot live more than three weeks without the energy you derive from eating food.
5. Three months for assistance: It is incredibly important to work with others whenever possible rather than going it alone.

SHOULD YOU STAY PUT OR SELF-RESCUE?

The hefty question posed in this subsection's title is rather easy to answer. In any situation where you are lost, your first thought should be to stay where you are. Set up a shelter, start a fire if needed and ensure you have plenty of water. Doing those three things will give you approximately three days to make a decision on whether you should effect a self-rescue.

If any of the following are true, you should stay put and follow the directions in the rest of this chapter to assist rescuers in finding you:

- You are unsure of your ability to accurately utilize your wilderness navigation skill set.

- You have an injury that is not life threatening.

- You have had little or no sleep.

- You are not adequately hydrated.

If any of the following are true, you may want to self-rescue:

- **You are traveling in area where there is no search-and-rescue service.** This is very rare in the United States. Outside of the US, there are many parts of the world that have no SAR service at all. You should know this before going into any area on adventure.

- **You are in immediate danger of certain death.** Injury or natural disaster has put you in a position where you know you are going to die without getting help within twenty-four hours. This may put you in a position where you will need to find safety away from the danger or be closer to medical attention when it arrives. Remember the Critical Rule of Three (see page 151), and take these into account. If you recall, core body temperature is the only issue that can cause immediate concern. If you don't have resources to maintain your core body temperature, it is best to make natural shelter to accomplish this. Here are some key points to help you do that:

- Get out of the wind and rain at all costs. Get behind rocks, trees, hills and other land features to avoid the wind. Seek out conifers to shed rain from you.

- Create a "squirrel's nest" of natural debris, branches, leaves, grass and other insulating elements to climb into like a squirrel does. This will keep many of the environmental conditions from affecting you.

- Use anything as an insulator from the ground. The ground will conduct what body heat you do have into the earth and away from you.

- **You have ignored every single piece of advice we have given you here and gone to an isolated area and absolutely no one knows you are gone or where you are traveling.** This is especially true if you have no vehicle at the starting point. An unattended vehicle will be noticed by authorities. If you were dropped off and no information about your trip was given to the driver, you are most likely not going to get help.

HOW TO SELF-RESCUE

Self-rescue can be a dangerous proposition even if you are well-hydrated and not injured. Follow these guidelines if you need to self-rescue:

- **Plan on attempting self-rescue during daylight hours, never at night.** Nighttime exponentially increases the likelihood of danger. We have had many students who came to us for survival training after such experiences. There have been many stories of people wandering in the dark, only to find that they were very close to the road, vehicle or other form of rescue and did not know it was there because they could not see.

- **Develop a plan before you go and stick to it.** The plan should include the direction you believe you should go and utilization of wilderness navigation skills to verify your location along the way. If you find things are not working out, you must stop what you are doing, because continuing will only make things worse.

- **Stop often to look at, listen to and smell your surroundings.** These senses will clue you in to rescuers, roads or other indicators of the civilized world.

- **Always consider yourself number one.** Keep yourself rested, hydrated and as calm as possible. Doing otherwise leads to poor decision making. You need all of your mental faculties to make good decisions in these circumstances.

COMMUNICATING FOR RESCUE

Communication for rescue goes way beyond your direct communication. It will often involve passive signaling with the hope that searchers can find you more easily. The most important aspect of signaling is to remember that you must stand out from your surroundings. You can do this by attracting the searchers' attention through their senses of sight, hearing and even smell. In the following section, we will show you how to increase the likelihood of being found.

The best mind-set is to think like the searchers do. Searchers will first go to the "last point seen" (LPS) and then to the "last known point" (LKP). (More often than not, these are not the same location, and the terms are used interchangeably. For instance, most often the place where your vehicle is parked is considered the LKP; however, if there are other hikers in the area, they may have seen you along a trail deep in the wilderness, so that will be the LPS.) Searchers will organize their members, make a plan and search for you. If you are moving during this time you are opening yourself up for injury or more danger. This will also make it harder for the searchers to find you. It is hard for you to hear or see them searching if you are on the move. Remember to stop and stay in place until they find you. See the sidebar for advice for children.

VISUAL SIGNALING

It is now time to "stand out from the crowd" more so than ever. You should view your surroundings and do all you can to look different from it. This should include being prepared if you wear camouflage or earth-toned clothing in the outdoors. Have other garments available to make yourself or your position more visible. I am a big fan of carrying a brightly colored bandana when I am out in wilderness areas. Bandanas have multiple uses, one of which is signaling.

In addition to using bright fabrics, review your surroundings for anything that might stand out from what is around and behind it. Metal cans, the dome of your flashlight, mirrors (such as in your compass) and anything that will reflect sunlight or man-made light is visible even during daylight hours. It is important to recognize that any sort of light that is steady is not as easily seen as one that goes on and off. The human eye is attracted to change. Your eye will more readily see something that flashes several times than something that stays on. You can enhance this reflection even further by understanding the international distress signal, which is anything that comes in threes.

WHAT DOES "HUG A TREE" HAVE TO DO WITH BEING LOST?

The Hug-a-Tree and Survive program was initiated by Ab Taylor for children between the ages of 7 and 11. At its core, the Hug-a-Tree and Survive program teaches participants to sit down close to a tree ("hugging" the tree) and stay in a location when they get lost. The beauty of the program is in its simple message, which is easy to retain and use under stress and which, in my estimation, makes it effective beyond that age group.

Since Taylor's passing, the program is now run by the National Association for Search and Rescue (NASAR). You can study and discover the program at NASAR's website (www.nasar.org). You can also become a presenter if that is your desire—you could teach material that might save a life someday.

Keep in mind that in a true survival situation, you should consider how many calories and how much water you will expend to get a signal. If the signaling is easy to accomplish, start early. If the signaling is difficult, ensure you have good shelter and water before pursuing it. Here are some examples of possible signaling devices:

Image 54: Swinging a chem light at night will provide an excellent visual indicator of your presence.

- Three campfires arranged in a triangular pattern.

- Three logs, rocks or piles of vegetation that differ in color from what they are lying on. For example, if you have three brown logs, lay them on green vegetation. If you have three piles of green vegetation, lay them on brown leaves, a sandy beach or similar terrain. Many suggest that you must put these items in a triangle, and there is absolutely nothing wrong with that. I queried both air and ground search-and-rescue personnel about this, and they each said they would be looking for anything out of the ordinary. A triangle or three items lying side by side would get their attention.

155

- Blink a flashlight in sequences of three. Note some flashlights come equipped to blink SOS in Morse code as well.

- Tie some cordage to a snaplight, and swing it in a circle at night to attract attention (see image 54). You can swing it vigorously for a short while, stop, swing it, stop, swing it, then take a longer break. This will equal three swings, which will again be a recognized as a distress signal.

- Create a flag with a stick and a brightly colored piece of clothing (another good use for that bandana).

There are some very important environmental conditions that you should be aware of when setting up any signal. Each of following presents its own challenges when you're trying to bring attention to your position:

- **Snowy conditions:** Don't assume a regular wood fire's smoke is going to bring visual attention to your position. Most smoke is white and will blend in with a snowy background. However, don't discredit a white-smoke fire in snow conditions altogether, as smoke can easily catch the attention of an SAR team in the area due to its scent. It also helps you maintain your core body temperature. To make a fire that will put off black smoke and is more easily seen against a snowy background, put an oil-based product on the fire. Oil or plastic are good choices. If you happen to be with your vehicle, seat covers or rubber floor mats are decent options. Some resinous trees will put off small amounts of black smoke, but it is not enough to warrant favoring these trees over other species. The woody portion of the tree is the part that is burning and making smoke, and it has very little oil in it to make a difference.

- **Wooded areas:** It is best if you find a clearing near your position for signaling. Fires, smoke and bright colors under a forested canopy are difficult for search teams to spot. Another good location is near waterways such as lakes, rivers or streams. Searchers will often focus on these areas and will be likely to find your signal along those routes.

- **Cloudy, overcast and foggy days:** These conditions make it difficult for searchers to locate you visually; however, with less sunshine, shiny objects will stand out more. Flashlights (or reflected light on a mirror, light shined up the bottom of a can and so on) are more easily seen in these conditions.

- **High mountainous terrain:** In large mountainous terrain, there is a higher likelihood of aircraft being used for the search. Increase your likelihood of being seen by placing signals on the top of ridgelines whenever possible.

There are some things you can do along the way to help if you ever get lost. If you are in a high–foot traffic area, it will be difficult for searchers to know if the marker was made by you or someone else. If you are going into a remote area via a known trail, or you are going off-trail, pointers (see image 55) are great ways to let others know your direction of travel.

At Nature Reliance School, we spend a great deal of time in the science and art of tracking. We train SAR, law enforcement and other first responders in this method of situational awareness. One thing we do is assist them in being what is accurately referred to as a "clue aware." This means not just simply *looking* at an area for signs and clues of passage, but *seeing* those indicators. The following methods are ways you can do this when you have no supplies (please note that some of these methods may go against the well-known Leave No Trace principles; it is our opinion that if you are certainly lost and in need of signaling for rescue and safety, the concept of Leave No Trace takes a back seat):

- Make a distinct and obvious set of tracks in an area that easily captures tracks. If good information was passed on to the SAR team looking for you, they may know what your track looks like.

- Break branches of surrounding trees when you leave a trail.

- When walking through tall grass, step on some of the grass rather than through or around it.

Image 55: Using natural materials will help you find areas and others find you, if needed.

CHOOSING THE BEST WOOD FOR SIGNAL FIRES

Woods used for signal fires come in two categories: sustainment and signaling. Let's look at each:

1. Sustainment: These are the woods that will burn long and slow, such as oaks, ash, hickory and hard maples. They will not put off significant flame for visual reference for searchers; however, they do make it less labor-intensive to keep a fire going. Once you get a fire going with these hardwoods, they don't require you to put more wood on often. When you need to amp up your fire for search crews, you can then add in some signaling woods.

2. Signaling woods: These are the woods that are less dense, such as most coniferous trees (pine, cedar, hemlock or spruce). These woods burn quick and hot. Because of this, they put off more flame, which in turn serves as an excellent light source for signaling.

Both types of wood mentioned are going to put off ample amounts of white smoke. None of them have enough oil to put off considerable black smoke for signaling against a white snowy background, though.

• If you are working through forest floor areas with lots of fallen leaves, then drag your foot occasionally to show that you have walked through the area.

• Remove bark from a tree to expose the light-colored area beneath the dark covering on the outside.

It bears repeating that the preceding methods are not stewardship-minded and go against Leave No Trace principles. These practices should be used only when you are lost and truly need assistance.

AUDIBLE SIGNALING

Before I begin explaining the audible options for signaling, I would like to point out that yelling or using a whistle will require you to expend a large amount of energy. You should use such options when you believe searchers or others are in the area. If you attempt to yell as soon as you realize you need rescue, you are expending calories at a time when no one can hear you.

Image 56: A whistle is a must-have for children and adults alike.

Here are some things you can use to attract attention through sound:

- **Voice:** Yell for help, and stop to listen often. Ground searchers will come through an area and yell your name. If you are yelling then you cannot hear them searching for you.

- **Whistle:** Using a whistle does not take as much energy as yelling, and the sound travels farther. Those are the reasons we believe whistles are an imperative piece of equipment to carry with you. We recommend putting them on a shoulder or sternum strap of your pack (see image 56) for easy access.

- **Hiking equipment:** Banging a pot or a pan that you have brought with you is another way to attract attention. Bear in mind that metal against metal will make a higher-pitched sound and that sound will travel farther.

SIGNALING EQUIPMENT AND TECHNOLOGY

There are several pieces of equipment that you can specifically bring on your wilderness adventure for signaling. The reason I have shared all the other signaling methods prior to these is the other methods never run out of batteries. Some of the following items will require batteries to work. Keep in mind our admonition in the preplanning section of this chapter (page 148) that anything that runs on batteries should be checked before you go *and* you should have backup batteries for field use:

- **Cell phone:** On many searches for a lost hiker, the lost person still has cell signal and can contact the proper authorities. The basic compass app on most cell phones, Google Maps and similar mapping programs provide the current position in terms of latitude and longitude. The best way to transfer this information is to take a screenshot and text it to the search team or dispatchers; however, you should assume that you will not have service in the backcountry and should not depend on a cell phone for rescue. If you must use a cell phone, you can climb to a high point of elevation to increase your chances of getting cell service if it does not put you in more danger to do so. Try texting someone for help. Texting only requires short intervals of connection to a cell tower to get the message across, whereas a phone call requires more. (Please also reference chapter 3, in which we discuss some useful apps for wilderness navigation.)

- **Flare:** These are probably not worth the weight for most people, but they do provide an excellent source of light. They can also help start survival fires in wet conditions.

- **Light beacon:** These are lights that when turned on, emit a steady blinking light. Beacons made for this purpose can run for several hours.

- **Personal locator beacons:** Personal locator beacons are one of those technological items that have been around for many years but are now completely affordable for the average hiker and backpacker. These devices utilize a high-frequency signal to send out a call of distress. This signal is received by three different agencies: (1) NOAA, (2) the Air Force Rescue Coordination Center and (3) the US Coast Guard. Note that some of the personal locator beacons currently available require you to have a monthly subscription or similar plan. Depending on the brand, they will send a message to a service provider who then contacts the proper responders. Some brands offer the option to send text messages along with the beacon.

- **Signal mirrors:** The majority of these have directions on the back for your use. I suggest getting one like that. They are simple to use, but it is rare that you will use one, so a refresher on the back is beneficial.

WHAT TO DO IF IT ALL GOES WRONG

TROUBLESHOOTING: OVERCOMING COMMON PROBLEMS WITH MIND-SET

The first third of this chapter can be summed up by saying you need proper mind-set. Each section contained its own way of handling problems such as normalcy bias, focus lock and so on. It bears repeating here that ego is the biggest problem for most people in the outdoors when it comes to fixing mistakes. You must admit as soon as possible that a mistake has been made and start to fix it. I always tell our students that failing does not make you a failure. That is where experience happens—"learn from your mistakes" is cliché but vital to the processing of wilderness navigation.

When it comes to troubleshooting the topics found in this chapter, consider the following:

- Preplanning is often overlooked, as many people feel that it detracts from the adventure of it all. Nothing can be further from the truth. Preplanning is vital to your continued success in the outdoors. The more you preplan, the safer you are. By being safer, even in dangerous activities, you can spend more time outside, go back home safely, then go back to do it again.

- If you get lost, the key is to stop what you are doing and take a break. Your physiological self is very strong under stress and will do things such as increase your heart rate, give an adrenaline dump and force auditory and visual exclusion in the effort to ensure your survival. The best way to combat this is to stop, sit down when possible and take a break. All of those physiological reactions are great to help you stay alive but they also put you in a position to make unwise decisions.

- Get out and practice with all your equipment so you know how well it is working before you need it. I always do a "mini run" of equipment before every trip.

QUESTIONS FOR PRACTICE

1. If you are venturing out on any hike, but especially a multiday hike, what is the first thing you should do?

2. When planning overnight camp areas, what map feature allows you to determine the slope?

3. Each of us are right- or left-foot dominant. What does this contribute to?

4. We are naturally predisposed to want things to be normal. What is this desire known as?

5. Focus lock will often do what?

6. What is the most natural state of an entire environment or a segment of an environment called?

7. What is the term used to describe anything that is a disruption to the baseline?

8. Take a look at the enclosed map. Imagine you need to find rubber or oil-based materials to start a fire. Where is the most likely place to find these when you are away from the roads?

9. If your navigation goes wrong, what is one of the first things you should do?

10. Creating a contrast between yourself and your surroundings will help you do what in an emergency?

11. Which uses less energy: yelling or using a whistle?

12. Open up the enclosed map on a table so you can see the whole thing. What areas would be good for signaling?

Answers: (1) Preplan. (2) Contour lines. (3) Drift. (4) Normalcy bias. (5) Keep us from observing what is going on around us. (6) Baseline. (7) Disturbance. (8) Along the shoreline of the lake. (9) Stop moving. (10) Be seen. (11) Using a whistle. (12) Two specific areas come to mind: (A) the hilltops throughout the area and (B) anywhere around the edge of the lake. These areas will allow you and any signal smoke you create to be seen from far away.

GET OUT AND PRACTICE

One of the best ways to get out and practice is to join your local search-and-rescue team. Most of these teams throughout the country readily accept volunteers. While it is a volunteer position, the whole team regularly gets together to train and work through problems.

The way we teach signaling in our classes is a great way for you to go about practicing, but it will require at least two people. Get a topography map of an area in which you can practice signaling both day and night. Use different types of signaling (e.g., start fires at night, create black-and-white smoke, use whistles and arrange signaling materials like stones and plants). Have your partner go 165 feet (50 m) out, 330 feet (100 m) out and beyond. (We will typically use radios to communicate while practicing. This allows both parties to communicate about what is happening and what they see, hear and smell and, perhaps more important, what they don't.) Ensure that you do this through open ground, through heavy cover and through all the different vegetation types that you recreate in. This practice exercise is incredibly enlightening as you learn what works and what does not.

Get out and play with fire. Not in a dangerous way but in a scientific, educational way. Study tree identification and get several different types of wood. Burn each type and note the following:

- [ ] How much smoke does it put off?
- [ ] How long does it take for it to catch fire?
- [ ] How long does it last in a sustained fire?
- [ ] How much heat does it put off? (You can test this by using a temperature gauge available at any home improvement store.)

You will start to develop a keen sense of how to use wood efficiently, especially for signaling. Reference page 158 for some helpful hints on species to get you started.

Reference the map that is enclosed. Note the areas on it that would be ideal positions for signaling (the highest hilltops, for example). If you were lost in this area, it would be one of the things that I'd start looking for when I have determined I need to stay put and signal for rescue. If there are any aircraft searching for you, look for spots that have less tree canopy above you so you are more easily seen.

NEXT-LEVEL SKILLS TO ROUND OUT YOUR KNOWLEDGE

In the previous section, we took you through the basic methods and processes of wilderness navigation. We also gave you the most helpful ways to troubleshoot these methods because they are so important. In this section, we want to round out the knowledge with some methods that are not typically taught in wilderness navigation. We want to guide you through these methods because we want you to use any and all available resources to navigate efficiently and safely.

Long before the map and compass were developed, humans discovered various ways of using the natural world to navigate the earth. While these methods have been used much longer than modern methods, we believe the modern navigator's skill should be improved and enhanced by these methods—they should not be the sole method of navigation. Learning how to recognize direction with the sky and land around us is definitely not time wasted. It does, however, take considerable effort and time in the field, which most individuals do not have. Therefore, we can employ our modern tools and use the methods described in this section to help verify what the modern tools tell us.

Note that it is the education aspect of the following chapters that you need to focus on. The "Troubleshooting" and "Get Out and Practice" sections will no longer be used in the rest of this book, because those aspects will be integrated into each section.

CHAPTER 6

USING THE DAY AND NIGHT SKY TO POINT YOU IN THE RIGHT DIRECTION

I know the stars are my home. I learned about them, needed them for survival in terms of navigation. I know where I am when I look up at the sky. I know where I am when I look up at the Moon; it's not just some abstract romantic idea, it's something very real to me. See, I've expanded my home. —Gene Cernan

History is a great teacher, and one source of inspiration for celestial navigation comes from the Phoenicians. The Phoenicians's civilization flourished due to their great trading ability and prime location in the eastern Mediterranean. They are commonly believed to have been the first people to recognize the North Star (also known as Polaris).

Around 1200 BC, the Phoenicians determined to expand their already budding trade routes by traveling via ships. Captains would stay close to the shorelines and only venture away from them when they knew they were in a direct line toward their intended target. They would eventually make it to the expected coastline, but they would often find themselves miles away from their destination. At some point close to 1100 BC, they determined that the North Star stayed in the same place in the sky at night. With this knowledge, they could keep the North Star directly behind or in front of their ships as they traversed the Mediterranean Sea along north-south shipping lanes. This kept the ships from getting lost at sea as well as on more direct lines with their intended destinations.

This seemingly small discovery was the key to helping the Phoenicians spread their trade routes as well as their culture, which included the Phoenician alphabet and ended the Greek Dark Age. This helped usher in the phase of history known as the Iron Age.

This story shows how important celestial navigation was to modern history. It was the beginning of navigation long before maps or compasses were made with great accuracy. In this chapter, we want to enhance your ability to navigate with something that never runs out of batteries, does not require magnetism, cannot get wet and shrivel up: celestial navigation.

Throughout this book, you may have noticed that we have stair-stepped our way into better and more accurate wilderness navigation methodology. Using the information in this and the next chapter is one more step in that direction. Two themes have run throughout this book. The first is the idea of wilderness navigation being a puzzle, and each time you add a piece to the puzzle, the clearer the picture becomes. The second is the idea of quality assurance in the process. Quality assurance in itself is a simple way of stating that we need efficiency, and we need accuracy. Before modern history, the use of the sky as a direction finder was imperative, as it was nearly all people had to do so. It worked well for that.

There are many things that give us direction in the sky. In the modern era, we must recognize that these things are the ultimate in quality assurance. A compass might spring, a map might get soaked, a GPS may run out of batteries—but Polaris is always going to be sitting above the North Pole. Use the items in this chapter to both enhance and be the final arbiter to your direction finding.

The day and night sky do not discriminate. All of us have experience with both. Where we find ourselves on this planet will greatly determine the way we view the sky and our ability to understand direction with it as well. It is best that we start by understanding the earth and its place in the solar system.

One of the most common navigational statements, "The sun rises in the east and sets in the west," is 100 percent false. The sun mostly just hangs out, does its thing and those of us here on Earth travel around it. It simply "appears" as if it rises in the east and sets in the west. Here are a few simple things that we should know before we use the day and night sky for navigation. You may have learned some of these in your school days, and the following are a nice refresher:

- The Northern Hemisphere (areas north of the equator) will see the noonday sun in the southern sky.

- We define our twenty-four-hour day based on the amount of time it takes for the earth to rotate along the poles.

- As we travel through a year of time, the area of the sky that we see the sun move through will change. For those of us in the Northern Hemisphere, the sun will be lower in the sky during the winter than it is during the summer. This forces the sun's rays to come in at a steeper angle. They then strike the ground and are more spread out and diluted. In the summer, they strike the ground in a more direct line, and that is why it is warmer in the summer.

- In late March and early September, the sun's path follows the celestial equator. It is then and only then that it rises directly east and sets directly west. The dates change each year but usually fall near March 20 and September 22 and are known as the equinoxes. It is on those days that day and night are of equal length.

- The time of year when the sun reaches its highest point is called the summer solstice, and the lowest point is called the winter solstice.

- The earth is tilted at 23.5 degrees as it relates to its orbit around the sun.

- The stars are much farther away than any distance you can move on Earth. Therefore, you will not be able to see them "move" in the sky just by changing position on Earth. It is important to understand that they do "move" very slowly throughout the night. The central point at which the stars "move" and rotate is known as the North Star. Bear in mind it is the Earth that is moving, not the stars themselves.

Ancient peoples designed whole cities and displays such as Stonehenge understanding the preceding celestial observations, as well as many others. Understanding celestial placements was such a fundamental part of life that civilizations strove to understand it throughout history. It was not until 300–200 BC that the Chinese determined you could use a naturally magnetized ore of iron called lodestone to develop what we now call a compass.

These celestial observations were of such importance that many aboriginal peoples wove fantastic legends into the cultural fabric based on their observations of the sky. Those stories were there to help them remember their history. They were also told so people would know the directions and how they related to an individual's position on the earth. Much like these cultures, we want to help you with some simple ways you can use the sky to get a general sense of direction, not an exact one.

THE SUN

As we established earlier, the sun appears to rise in the east and set in the west. Knowing that will allow us to use the sun to determine direction. Many people have unknowingly assumed the shadow-stick (see image 57) method is an accurate method for all locations and all times of the year. That is not true. It is an accurate method as long as we put it under certain constraints. The original thought is that if you take a straight stick and place it in the ground, it will cast shadows when the sun hits it. It will cast a westward shadow past the stick when it is in the east and an eastward shadow past the stick when it is in the west. The reason this method is inaccurate is because the tilt of the earth during various times of year places the sun at an angle so as to not cast shadows in this way.

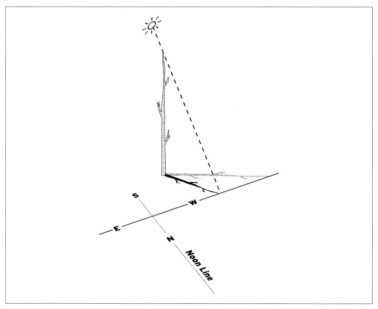

Image 57: Using a shadow stick for east-west approximation is an innacurate tool many times of the year.

NOON IS NOT WHAT YOU THINK IT IS

It's common knowledge that 12:00 p.m. is the time of day we typically refer to as noon. A more important understanding is when midday is. This is the point of the day when the sun is at its peak. This means the sun is directly due south (for those of us in the Northern Hemisphere). This does not always occur at exactly 12:00 p.m. For thorough understanding, it is necessary to recognize the position of the sun first and the time of day secondarily. This is because our timekeeping is very exact, but it is a contrived understanding to the movement of the sun. Pay attention to the sun to determine midday, which is when it is at its highest point.

Take, for example, the solstices. Due to the sun being at its highest or lowest point, the accuracy of the shadow decreases. This inaccuracy can be as much as 30 degrees through the course of the day. What we also know is that inaccuracy goes to nearly zero the closer we are to noon. This means to make this method a more accurate representation of an east-west line, it would be best to mark a certain amount of time before noon (e.g., one hour before), and then take another reading at the same reference time after noon (e.g., one hour after noon). By making your marks at 11:00 a.m. and 1:00 p.m., you span the time frame when it is most accurate and can, therefore, get a general sense of the east-west line.

We don't typically like to cover topics that do not work very well. But we have done that with the shadow-stick method because it has been taught and retaught so many times that it is taken as complete truth. It was worth our time to share with you why and how it is inaccurate. What we can do with the shadow-stick method is find a very accurate north-south line (see image 58). Follow these steps to do so:

- Choose a level area of ground where it is easy to see the shadows. Exposed dirt or sand is a good choice.

- Place a stick in the ground at 90 degrees to the ground itself.

- Observe the shadow the stick makes on the ground.

- Mark the end of the shadow with a small rock or similar item. Ensure that the marks are made before, during and after midday.

You will notice that the marks form a curve that resembles a U with the bottom of the U close to the stick. The spot you marked closest to the stick is on the north-south line. This occurs because the sun is directly in the southern sky and is at its highest point at midday, causing it to cast a very short shadow that lies directly north of the stick.

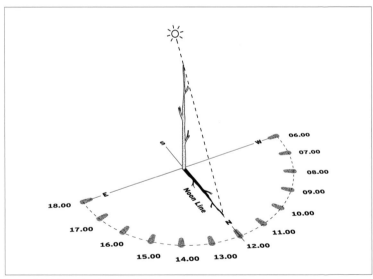

Image 58: Using the shadow stick for north-south appoximation is a much better use of this knowledge.

THE MOON

The moon has the important job of controlling the ocean tides and helping various plants grow. It is for good reason that we should pay attention to the moon. There are three methods by which we can utilize the moon, or its phases, to tell us direction.

METHOD 1: OBSERVING A CRESCENT MOON

The easiest way we can utilize the moon for direction is to consult it during a crescent phase. The two horns (sometimes called points) of the crescent moon help us determine direction. Draw an imaginary line from the top horn down through the bottom horn and continue that line to the horizon. Where that line intersects the horizon will be south for us in the Northern Hemisphere. As you may already suspect, this is the general direction of south (see image 59).

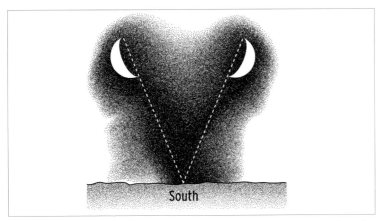

Image 59: The horns of the crescent moon will point toward the horizon where due south is.

METHOD 2: USING A SHADOW STICK

Another method is to observe the moon over a long period of time. The moon is similar to the sun in that it will rise and set in an east-to-west arc. Keep in mind that it does not rise and set exactly as the sun does. Knowing the phases of the moon (see image 60) is helpful, but note that the moon does not need to be completely full to use a shadow stick (see page 172) to get a sense of direction. It does, however, need to be bright.

During the moon's arc, it will be at its highest point when it crosses over the meridian line that you are on (see chapter 1). When this occurs, the moon is due south of you and will make the shortest shadow with the shadow stick. I had heard of this concept for many years before trying it while writing this book. I found that it worked well, but it required a clear night with a bright moon to make a shadow.

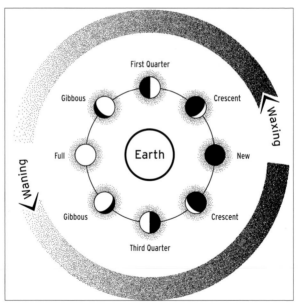

Image 60: Understanding moon phases is valuable to understanding the sun's movement and its east-west indication.

METHOD 3: USING MOON PHASES

The moon goes through phases in a cycle (see image 60). You must first understand the terms waxing and waning. Waxing is the time between a new moon and a full moon. This is when the visible size of the moon is increasing. The waning period is the time after the full moon and before the new moon. The visible size of the moon is decreasing during this time. (One way of remembering the term *waxing* is to think of it like waxing a car: When the moon is waxing, that is when it is getting brighter.)

When the moon is waxing, it will be following the sun as it arcs across the sky. Since it is following the sun, the moon's western side will be illuminated.

When the moon is waning, it will be leading the sun as it arcs across the sky. Since it is now leading the sun, its eastern side will be illuminated.

All that precedes is to say you should always be cognizant of the phase the moon is currently in. Those who spend a great deal of time in the wilderness regularly pay attention to weather patterns, moon phases and other indicators. By knowing the moon is in a waning phase, for example, you can roughly identify east and west because the eastern side is illuminated.

THE STARS

The sun and the moon provide a general sense of direction. Sailors have utilized the stars for more exact navigation for hundreds of years. Yet navigating by the stars requires some equipment, such as a transit, that the typical wilderness navigator does not carry. Thankfully, the stars still offer us more accurate navigation opportunities even without such equipment.

THE NORTH STAR IN THE NORTHERN HEMISPHERE

If you were to extend the North Pole into the cosmos, it would nearly run into the North Star (also called Polaris). The North Star will give those of us in the Northern Hemisphere a great sense of where due north is. Locating it is rather easy as well. It has been suggested by many that the North Star is the brightest star in the night sky. This may be true some parts of the year, but not always. For example, one of the brightest objects in the sky at the time of this writing is the International Space Station. Follow the following three steps so you can more accurately find the North Star:

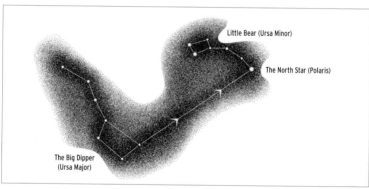

Image 61: You can use the Big Dipper to find the North Star (Polaris).

- If you are a first-timer trying to find the North Star, get your compass out and locate north. This will help focus your attention on the part of the night sky that contains the North Star. Once you learn how to find it, you will most likely not need the compass anymore.

- Search for the Big Dipper (see image 61). This is a constellation that looks much like a scoop or dipper. It has three stars that make up the handle and four that make up the dipping cup.

- Draw an imaginary line from the bottom end of the dipper through the top end of the dipper and continue that line outward. Use your outstretched fingers to measure along that imaginary line. You will find the North Star on that line approximately 3½ hands from the top portion of the dipper. You will also find that the North Star is the last star in the handle of the Little Dipper.

CONSTELLATIONS: THERE IS AN APP FOR THAT

Maneuvering your way through all the stars and constellations out there is a daunting task. Technology that helps you navigate the night sky makes stargazing easier and a lot more fun. Following is a list of the top five most-downloaded apps for stargazing. Pick one of these up and you will never look at the night sky the same again:

1. Sky Guide: This is the one I use—it displays all the stars, planets and satellites and helps me recognize the constellations associated with them.

2. SkyView®: This is a good all-in-one app for stargazing.

3. Night Sky: This is a great app that uses the iOS system to create a nice augmented-reality sky map.

4. Star Walk: This app includes excellent views of stars and planets along with some mythological stories of the celestial sky.

5. NASA: This is the official app that keeps you up-to-date on all the latest space news.

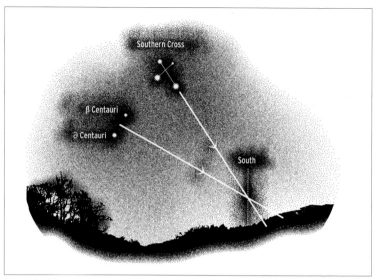

Image 62: You can use the Southern Cross and pointer to find direction as well.

THE SOUTHERN CROSS IN THE SOUTHERN HEMISPHERE

The North Star is great and all, but it does not help our friends down south too much. There is not an equivalent "South Star" that can be easily seen by the naked eye. What our friends in the Southern Hemisphere do have is the Southern Cross. Still, it is not as easy to utilize as the North Star and the Big Dipper in helping with navigation. The Southern Cross (see image 62) will move across the sky and is a useful navigational aid only when it appears to be vertical in the sky. When it is vertical, the longer portion of the cross points to within 3 degrees of south. This constellation stays visible longer the closer you get to the South Pole. This prolonged visibility occurs during a short window from May to June each year. During the rest of the year, you can still use the Southern Cross, but you must add in the pointer stars as well.

LEFT, UP, RIGHT, DOWN (LURD)

Left, Up, Right, Down (LURD) is one of those hidden gems in the wilderness navigation world. We first read of this acronym in the book *The Essential Wilderness Navigator* (see our appendix of suggested resources on page 264 for this and other wilderness navigation resources). The beauty of LURD is that you do not have to have a full view of the night sky to use it as a navigational aid. If it's a clear night, and you can see some stars, but trees or other features are covering the Big Dipper and North Star, this method will come in handy. LURD is an acronym that, when properly associated with the four cardinal directions and direction references, will help you know what direction you are heading. Please reference the following table and image 63 to see how to utilize LURD.

N	L	North = Left
E	U	East = Up
S	R	South = Right
W	D	West = Down

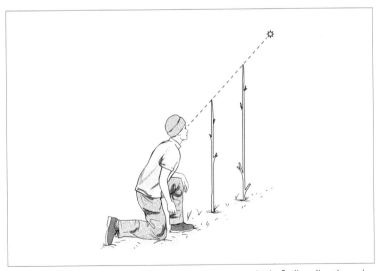

Image 63: Sighting over two sticks, or even trees, can assist in finding direction using any star.

You can use any geographical feature (such as a mountaintop or obvious tree), or you can use sticks as shown in the photo on page 179. Follow these steps to find the direction you are facing at the time you look over the "sight" (note that this process works best in the Northern Hemisphere):

- Find a spot where you can see some visible stars. This can be in the open or through a small hole in a forest canopy.

- Set your tallest pole or stick farthest from your position, approximately 5 feet (1.5 m) away from the other pole or stick.

- Set a shorter pole closer to your current position.

- Use the poles to line up your sight and pick a star that sits atop the tall pole directly on that line of sight. I typically squat down to do this.

- Keep your eye on that star and wait a minimum of fifteen minutes.

- Once the time has passed, note where the star has moved from its original position.

- You can now determine the direction you are facing during this exercise. If the star moved left, you are facing north; if the star moved up, you are facing east; if the star moved right, you are facing south; and if the star moved down, you are facing west.

As we noted earlier, the stars revolve around the North and South Poles. Since they are closer to the poles, this exercise is best done with a star that appears closer to the horizon. The stars closest to the poles will not appear to move as much and their movement will be harder to decipher.

Many people in the modern world think that methods of celestial navigation like we just discussed are a bit too "out there" for their liking. What if you could look at the plants and trees around you to assist you in navigation? In chapter 7, we are going to do exactly that.

QUESTIONS FOR PRACTICE

1. True or false: For those in the Northern Hemisphere, the arc of the sun will be lower and shorter during the winter than during the summer.

2. True or false: In the Northern Hemisphere, the sun will always appear to rise exactly due east and set exactly due west.

3. What is another name for the North Star?

4. The North Star is in what constellation?

5. The spring and fall equinoxes each have two unique features. What are they?

6. What does LURD stand for?

7. Can we use a crescent moon to give accurate direction?

8. Approximately how many "hands" is the North Star from the cup of the Big Dipper?

9. Why is the shadow-stick method a suspect method of direction finding?

10. On the summer _____ the sun is at its _____, and on the winter _____ the sun is at its _____ point in the sky.

Answers: (1) True. (2) False. (3) Polaris. (4) The Little Dipper. (5) The day and night are of equal length of time; the sun will "rise" exactly due east and "set" exactly due west. (6) Left, Up, Right, Down: Left = north, up = east, right = south, down = west. (7) No. (8) 3½. (9) Using a crescent moon will give us only a general understanding of south. (10) Depending on the time of year, the tilt of the earth can skew the stick's findings. Solstice; highest; solstice; lowest.

CHAPTER 7

UTILIZING FLORA AND FAUNA FOR GENERAL NAVIGATION NEEDS

It should be expected that we will find wonder in a vast mountain landscape, but it is a more serious challenge to find wonder in a hill. It is a great achievement to find it in a molehill. —Tristan Gooley

Riccarda Balogh's story of survival is nothing short of incredible. In 1956, she, along with several friends, fled her native Hungary to save their own lives in the midst of the nationwide revolt against the Marxist-Leninist government and its Soviet-imposed policies.

Up until that moment, they were all twenty-something adults with no regular experience with or education in cross-country travel. They determined it would be best for them to attempt to make it to Yugoslavia and its relative safety. Balogh had hidden away a small button compass to assist them in their escape. To keep as low a profile as possible, they would travel only during darkness and hide during the day. They used matches under their coats to view the compass at regular intervals.

Riccarda and her companions also used the various terrain and vegetative features along the way to stay on their intended heading toward Yugoslavia. By recognizing directions from trees outlined by the night sky, they could continue to verify their location along the way with the tiny compass. At one point they encountered a bog that they knew was run off from a nearby waterway, which was an indicator they were close to Yugoslavia. Recognition of different natural elements, in the dark, was one way they were able to navigate without the aid of modern equipment and without looking at the compass repeatedly by the light of the matches. To do so in that war-torn area could have easily compromised their location.

You may have concluded from our discussion in chapter 6 about using celestial bodies as navigation aids that an astronomer would be a good person to share a campfire with. They are the specialists when it comes to such things. The topic we address in this chapter is no different. If you get an opportunity to walk the woods with a forest ecologist, wildlife or plant biologist or a forester, don't miss it. These people are invaluable in enhancing your knowledge of all things outdoors and can specifically assist you with wilderness navigation as well.

Learning from someone else is how I was introduced to the topic of utilizing trees in determining direction. I am heavily involved in doing wildlife habitat improvement on private property. I enjoy working with the environment, especially forested areas, in an effort to increase natural nesting and feeding opportunities for wildlife. One piece of property that I work on regularly (and that I now sit on to write this book) provided an opportunity for a Kentucky Division of Forestry forester to teach me some valuable lessons. The property had been very poorly logged about twenty-five years prior to my owning it. The forester advised that one way to improve its health was to clear-cut a hillside. I asked him why that particular hillside and he said, without batting an eye, "Based on its direction to the sun." Clear-cutting would encourage oak, and other wildlife-friendly species would grow there. He also showed me that if another hillside were clear-cut, it would come back in only pines, which are not as valuable to wildlife habitat improvement. Up to that point, I was not aware there is so much order when it comes to what trees grow in an area. I thought it was all rather random. That was twenty-five years ago. I have spent the better part of my time since then learning and experiencing things that were previously unseen by me. There is much order to a wilderness environment, and it is something that we can utilize to help us determine direction.

By now, I am sure you can see that doing wilderness navigation correctly is an exercise of situational awareness. Recognizing what is going on around you at any given time is an opportunity to not only navigate safely but also enjoy your surroundings even more. Utilizing trees and plants for navigational needs is one way to enhance your experience and stay safe at the same time. Always remember that wilderness navigation is a puzzle. Putting the puzzle pieces together to assimilate a recognizable image is the goal. To get there, it sometimes requires you to look closely at an individual piece and see if it matches with something that is missing. Utilizing plants and trees around us is no different. It will require you to pay special attention to species, how they grow, their placement on the earth and much more.

MOSS DOES NOT ALWAYS GROW ON THE NORTH SIDE OF TREES

"Moss always grows on the north side of trees." Let's go ahead and dispense with this tidbit of false information right here. We have heard this oft-repeated phrase time and time again by the recreational adventurist. Like most "rules" of this nature, there is a small amount of solid reasoning for why so many people believe this. To understand why this misconception is not true, we must first understand moss.

Our friend moss likes to drink. So much so that it enjoys growing in dark, damp and shady places. Any spot that is shaded and damp will then be more likely to contain moss than a spot where you find direct sunlight. Recall from chapter 6 that for those of us in the Northern Hemisphere, the sun travels through the southern sky. This means that the north side of trees tend to be more shaded than the other sides, which will be subject to more direct sunlight. This is what we need to pay special attention to. For trees that stand alone in an open area, their exposure to the sun is determined only by the sun itself. In a wilderness setting, it is entirely different. In a wilderness environment, sunlight falls on the forest floor only in places where the upper canopy allows it to go. That upper canopy of a forest is often starved for sunlight, so it gobbles it up whenever it can. This upper canopy casts shadows nearly everywhere. Some of those shadows will be there throughout the year, even in a deciduous wilderness (i.e., in which trees drop their leaves every year). If a spot stays shaded due to the tree canopy, it will contain more moisture. It is there that the moss will be most likely to flourish—even if it is on the south, east or west side of a tree.

TREES AND SUNLIGHT

In a wooded environment, trees can tell us a lot about direction. Unlike moss (see the sidebar on page 185), trees enjoy the sunlight. But there is a distinction between those that *love* sunlight and those that *like* it. Trees that cannot get enough sunlight are often referred to by forestry professionals as shade-intolerant. These are trees that do not like a lot of competition for the sun. Those species that do not mind a little competition and do very well in shaded areas are referred to as—you guessed it—shade-tolerant species.

You may be asking yourself why this distinction even matters. Refer to page 171, where we discuss the arc of the sun in the southern sky. Isolated trees that are shade-intolerant will often have branches that are "heavy" on the south side of the tree. Take a look at image 64. What you see in this image is a larger number of branches on the south side of the tree. This is because the south side of that tree receives more sunlight. The tree "knows" this and will put out more branches on that side in order to gather sunlight. You will also notice that on the north side of the trees the branches reach up rather than out toward the sun. In his exhaustive work entitled *The Natural Navigator*, Tristan Gooley refers to this as "Check Effect." This means that branches on the south side of the tree reach out and the branches on the north side grow vertically, forming a check-mark shape. We can apply this same process to a whole hillside of trees as it relates to shade-tolerant and shade-intolerant species.

Image 64: The "heavy" side of an isolated tree will often be on the south side.

Imagine you have a hillside that faces the southern sky. That hillside will receive more sunlight than a hillside facing the northern sky. It is on that south-facing hillside (i.e., more sunlight) that you often find a bigger collection of shade-intolerant species (i.e., ones that dislike shade and prefer lots of sun). On the north-facing hillside (i.e., less sunlight) you will find a bigger collection of shade-tolerant species (i.e., ones that prefer shade and dislike sun).

The following tables provide a listing of the most common shade-tolerant and shade-intolerant trees in North America.

Most Common Shade-Tolerant Trees in North America	
Common Name	Scientific Name
Boxelder	Acer negundo
Sugar maple	Acer saccharum
Buckeye	Aesculus spp.
Flowering dogwood	Cornus florida
Persimmon	Diospyros spp.
American beech	Fagus grandifolia
American holly	Ilex opaca
White spruce	Picea glauca
Black spruce	Picea mariana
Red spruce	Picea rubens
American basswood	Tilia americana
Northern white cedar	Thuja occidentalis
Red mulberry	Morus rubra
American hornbeam	Carpinus caroliniana
Southern magnolia	Magnolia grandiflora
Eastern hemlock	Tsuga canadensis
Tupelo	Nyssa spp.

Most Common Shade-Intolerant Trees in North America	
Common Name	Scientific Name
Paper birch	Betula papyrifera
Catalpa	Catalpa spp.
Pecan	Carya illinoinensis
Kentucky coffee tree	Gymnocladus dioicus
Butternut	Juglans cinerea
Black walnut	Juglans nigra
Eastern red cedar	Juniperus virginiana
Yellow poplar	Liriodendron tulipifera
Osage-orange	Maclura pomifera
Shortleaf pine	Pinus echinata
Longleaf pine	Pinus palustris
Red pine	Pinus resinosa
Pitch pine	Pinus rigida
Loblolly pine	Pinus taeda
Virginia pine	Pinus virginiana
Sycamore	Platanus occidentalis
Eastern cottonwood	Populus deltoides
Bigtooth aspen	Populus grandidentata
Quaking aspen	Populus tremuloides
Pin cherry	Prunus pensylvanica
Black cherry	Prunus serotina
Black locust	Robinia pseudoacacia
Willow	Salix spp.
Sassafras	Sassafras spp.

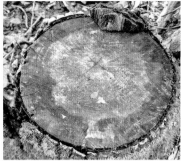

Image 65: On the left of this photo, you see pine trees and on the right, you see deciduous trees. This is because of the amount of sunlight each side receives.

Image 66: Rings will be thicker (pictured on bottom here) on the south side of an isolated tree.

Let's look at a real-life example using the information presented in the preceding tables. There is small wildlife opening in front of me as I write this (see image 65). On the south side of the field, you can see a number of shade-intolerant Virginia pine; on the north side, you can see mostly shade-tolerant maples and flowering dogwoods. Just by simply walking into this opening, someone with this small bit of understanding could see the general direction of things. You may recall from the sidebar about moss (page 185) that sunlight is hard to come by on the forest floor and all sides of a tree where there are many trees. That is why an opening in the woods—not necessarily in a forested area—is where you can get this type of information.

TREE STUMPS

There are very few old-growth forests in existence today. Nearly all have been host to logging operations. It is on these sites that you will find the stumps of felled trees. We enjoy stopping and counting the rings when we can to see how old the trees were when they were cut. We can assume that, all things being equal—such as nutrition, minerals in the soil, available sunlight and activity level in the area—a tree similar in diameter to a stump that is nearby is close to the same age. As you look closely at the rings, you will often notice that one side of the tree has thicker rings (see image 66). It is on that side that the tree has taken in more sunlight and has therefore grown more. In the Northern Hemisphere, this means that that side of the tree is south.

WIND EFFECTS

In our estimation, utilizing the wind as a navigation tool will require you to understand the prevailing winds of a place. A good way to understand these winds in general is to have a weathervane around your home. There are electronic ones now that will detail wind, rain and barometric pressure. If you discipline yourself to regularly notice the wind's direction, you will develop a sense of it and you will notice it subconsciously. You can also look at the radar on your favorite TV weather report or app. This will give you a quick sense of prevailing winds. It is easy to see patterns that emerge. For example, in central Kentucky where we live, most of the weather patterns come out of the southwest and travel northeast. This sort of patterning works even better where you have open ground, such as plains, desert or large and open unforested areas.

You should also notice that much of this information on wind will change in areas with significant mountains or hills. While there are still prevailing winds, large mountains and hills can stop winds due to their sheer size, and the wind will travel the path of least resistance. This means that valleys and features such as rivers will be likely to carry winds no matter what the prevailing winds of that area are.

Understanding these wind patterns can help with navigation because regular wind patterns will force the environment around you to shift. This means we have several navigational aids that are easy to discern in a wilderness thanks to the wind:

Image 67: Prevailing winds will force leaves, snow and other debris to gather on the downwind side of stumps and trees.

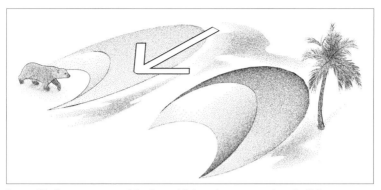

Image 68: Open areas containing loose debris such as snow and sand will form crescent shapes based upon wind patterns.

- Leaves and forest debris will pile up on the sheltered side of a tree. If the wind is blowing from west to east, then leaves will accumulate on the east side of a tree, away from the wind (see image 67).

- Sand, snow and loose dirt will form a U shape with the bottom of the U crescent facing the wind. The side facing the wind will have a slope that slowly rises to the top, whereas the bowl side of the crescent will be steep. In our example, if the wind is blowing from west to east, the bottom of the crescent will be facing west (see image 68).

- Pick up a handful of loose, dry forest debris such as grass or leaves. Toss it into the air and watch the direction the wind carries it.

- Wet your finger and hold it up in the air. You will feel the body heat leaving your finger when it is in the direction of the wind. It will feel cooler than the other fingers. This method is a simple classic, but it works.

PLANTS

Another misunderstanding regarding nature awareness is that flowering plants always face the sun. This is often stated about sunflowers. But it's not true. I used to raise many acres of sunflowers. The ones I raised, and others that I have researched, would most often face east. There are many species of flowers like this. These flowers really enjoy following the sun as it comes up, but not all day. They will face east and gather plenty of sunlight, facing the sun for a while, but often stop their chase around midday.

There are a few flowers that will track along with sun from sunup to sundown. Phlox, which can be found in wilderness areas, will face the sun all day. Much like the shadow-stick method we discussed earlier (see page 170), if you see phlox facing the sun at midday, the direction it is facing is due south.

In desert environments, you can see this preference for flowers facing the sun on the giant cactus. Giant cacti have a flowering portion that most often grows on the southeastern side. Since the desert gets cold at night, the flowers will go nearly dormant and rise up to gather sunlight first thing in the morning.

Due to their delicate nature, the seeds of flowering plants and reeds will grow away from the prevailing wind direction. For reeds, this means the plume primarily grows on the sheltered side of the reed itself. Another plant that many are familiar with is the dandelion. You most likely know that a dandelion will have a white head when it is time to broadcast its seeds. Because you are developing your situational awareness, you will notice the dandelion is missing one side of its seed head. The side where the seeds are missing is where the prevailing winds come from. If you already know the direction of the prevailing winds of that area, you can then have an approximation of direction.

THE LAND

Nature Reliance School is well known for our instructors' ties to tracking. Tracking in and of itself is situational awareness at a heightened state. That sounds familiar within the confines of this current subject matter, doesn't it? One thing we spend a lot of our time doing when we're tracking is looking at track traps. Track traps are places where it is easy for the ground to capture and hold tracks. Several examples are features favorable to mud, such as roads, puddles and stream banks. After noting these sorts of "track traps" over many years, it became apparent that the south-facing side of muddy ground dries

before the north-facing side. This is because the south-facing side gets more sunlight (see image 69). As with all of these natural navigation methods, there are many variables that must be considered. I would not use dried mud in a single puddle as my go-to directional tool. If I have other tools, such as map or compass, I could use the dried mud as a quality-control measure to verify accuracy of my equipment. If no tools are available, I would only use it in concert with several other indicators. For example, I would look at a wildlife opening, the heavy side of a tree and a mud puddle before even considering the approximate direction for wilderness navigation.

Image 69a: The south-facing side of a puddle will dry faster, due to it receiving more sunlight.

Snow is a good indicator of direction as well. If you are looking at a valley or hollow that runs east to west, the south-facing hillside will melt quicker than the north-facing side. This is much like the principle of shade-tolerant versus shade-intolerant species of trees we discussed on page 187. Another instance of direction finding with snow follows the premise of snow blowing with the prevailing wind. When the wind blows hard or the snow is quite "sticky," it will stick to the side of trees facing the prevailing wind. If you know the direction the winds typically travel, this will give you a general sense of direction.

In these preceding two chapters, we have considered our natural surroundings as they pertain to wilderness navigation. It bears repeating that most of these methods are best considered ways to obtain a general sense of direction. They certainly do help us with quality control of that wilderness navigation puzzle we are putting together. If you are trekking along an azimuth and you come across one of these natural navigation helps, don't dismiss it. We have covered only a handful of the various nature-based methods. By utilizing your map, compass and GPS on your regular adventures, you are sure to come up with some methods of your own. That is one more reason for you to spend more time outside!

Image 69b: Understanding prevailing wind and weather patterns will help you understand direction when looking at snow indicators.

QUESTIONS FOR PRACTICE

1. True or false: If you see moss growing on a tree, the side the moss is growing on is north.

2. How does the sun affect tree growth and how does this apply to direction finding?

3. Will trees typically have more or fewer branches facing south?

4. As you look closely at the rings of a stump, you will often notice that one side of the tree has thicker rings. In the Northern Hemisphere, this means that side of the tree is facing which direction?

5. Snow is a good indicator of direction. For example, if you are looking at a valley or hollow in the Northern Hemisphere that runs east to west, will the snow on the south-facing hillside or the north-facing hillside melt first?

6. Blowing leaves will often accumulate on which side of a tree?

7. To first utilize wind as a navigation tool you must understand the _____ winds of the areas.

8. Why aren't sunflowers a good flower to utilize for direction finding at any time of day?

9. What is a track trap and how can it be used to tell direction?

10. What does it mean if a tree is shade-tolerant?

Answers: (1) False. Moss grows on the side with the most moisture, which is not necessarily north. (2) All plants grow heavier on the side facing the sun. If a tree growing isolated in the open is heavier on one side, it is highly probable that it is the south-facing side. (3) More in the Northern Hemisphere. (4) South. (5) South-facing. (6) The sheltered side. (7) Prevailing. (8) They will face the southeast only until about midday. (9) Track traps are places where it's easy for the ground to capture and hold tracks. The side of the trap that's drier indicates that it's the side that gets the most sun. If this is found in an open area, it is most likely the south-facing side. (10) It means that the tree will grow well in the shade.

CHAPTER 8

USING EIGHTH-GRADE MATH SKILLS TO NAVIGATE LIKE A BOSS

I think the universe is pure geometry—basically, a beautiful shape twisting around and dancing over space-time. —Garrett Lisi

All good teachers should continue to be good students. That is why Tracy and I continually train and challenge each other. We also regularly train with other teachers.

Many years ago, Tracy and I traveled to another state to do some land navigation training under another instructor. While we were en route, the instructor called us and asked if we would be interested in doing the land navigation course in conjunction with an active search he was involved in. We jumped at the chance and got involved in the search as soon as we showed up on the scene. We spent two days searching and, unfortunately, our search revealed only one sign that was not already discovered. It was evident from information gathered at the scene that the lost person intended on going into the woods to commit suicide. Finding the person alive was a foregone conclusion. Finding his body was something that needed to be done to help bring closure to the family as well as properly gather his body for burial.

I was sent the AAR later, after the body was discovered. The searchers, after recognizing the search was a body recovery rather than an active search for rescue, utilized a rectangular search pattern. They first used the outer limits of the search area in an effort to ensure that the person's body was inside the containment area. They then walked straight lines along the outer portion, turned 90 degrees and walked the next outer portion. After completing the first rectangle, the searchers would step in 3 feet (1 m) and walk another rectangle inside the first. This procedure created an ever-shortening search area that was checked in every crevice, hollow, creekbed and beyond. Having employed this search pattern, searchers came upon the area where the person had crawled under an overhanging rock, covered himself up with leaves and then ended his life. He had chosen to conceal himself in an effort to not be found, which, had the searchers not been successful, would have caused untold turmoil in his family.

Searchers employing a rectangular search pattern and using compasses to turn 90 degrees were able to bring the search to a close.

As you may have noticed, there is a bit of mathematics involved in wilderness navigation. If you start to dig deep into astronomy and celestial navigation, you can get heavily involved in calculus, trigonometry and other hefty math concepts that are difficult to utilize on the move in a wilderness. We want to avoid that. There are many very simple and practical geometry lessons that you most likely learned as far back as eighth grade that we can utilize in our land navigation learning.

FINDING YOURSELF BY TRIANGULATION

We have taught a range of youth programs for Nature Reliance School and one thing always stands out when we are teaching them: There is a tremendous amount of self-discovery going on within the minds of middle school students. They are truly trying to find themselves before navigating further on the trail of life. How ironic it is that we can use some of the things that age group learns in math class to also help all of us, youths and adults alike, navigate in the wilderness.

One of the first things you should be able to do is to find your position on a map within a wilderness setting. A simple way to do this is to find various lines that indicate your position on the earth in front of you and on the map you have in your hands. Here are the steps to accomplish this without a compass (see image 70):

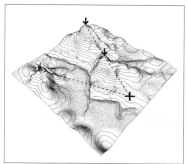 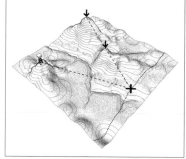

Image 70: Use multiple land features even without a known feature, such as a trail, to triangulate your position.

Image 71: Use two in-line features (see line on right) and a known feature, such as a trail, to find your locations.

- Look out and in front of you for two land features that line up with your current position.

- Now find the same two features on your map. Draw a line that extends from the two features toward your position on the map.

- Turn your body and do the same thing again with two different land features.

- Draw a line on your map that connects the second two land features and your direction of position on the map.

- Where those two lines intersect is where you are in relation to the map.

- You can now utilize terrain association to continue your travel.

The preceding steps can be difficult to accomplish, because it requires so many geographic features to line up in a certain way. Although it is possible, it would be difficult at best to find that many features in that specific arrangement. This is just one more reason why having a compass is a game changer. By utilizing it properly, we can find ourselves in the right area by using two recognizable features. Take a look at image 71 and follow these steps:

- Find a recognizable land feature in front of you.

- Utilize your compass to take an azimuth to that feature. Refer back to chapter 2 for directions on how to take an appropriate azimuth. (Remember this is a magnetic reading.)

- Adjust your compass for declination going to your map. (See chapter 1 for information on declination.)

- Lay the edge of your compass on your map with one edge of your compass intersecting the recognizable feature. Use that feature as your pivot point until Red Fred is in the Shed (see page 54 if you need a refresher).

- Draw a line along the edge of your compass.

- If you are on a recognizable linear feature (such as a river or valley), your position is where the line intersects the feature.

- If you are not on such a feature (for example, if you are in the middle of an open field), then find another recognizable feature elsewhere. You will follow the same steps as described in the preceding bullets on this second feature. Draw your angle from that feature. Your position is where the two lines intersect.

DETERMINING DISTANCES WITH TRIANGLES

Pythagoras devised a remarkable theorem that bears his name: the Pythagorean theorem. As a refresher, the Pythagorean theorem of right triangles states that the hypotenuse (the side opposite the right angle) is equal to the sum of the squares of the other two sides (see image 72).

The theorem allows us to give an approximate distance between a certain location and a geographic feature on a map. From a central point at which two sides of the triangle create a right angle, we can take an azimuth in one direction, turn 90 degrees and take another. We can then venture out a known distance on those lines. By relying on our knowledge of the Pythagorean theorem and by walking a known distance, we can then determine the distance between the ending point of line X and line B (see image 73).

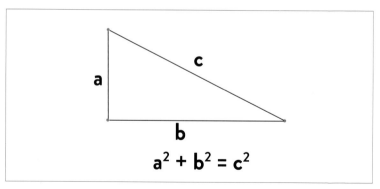

Image 72: The Pythagorean theorem

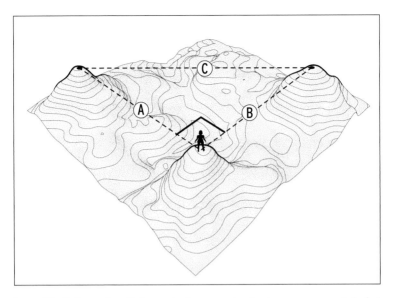

Image 73: Understanding Pythagoras's theorem and using it on a map can help find approximate distances and angles.

The obvious question here is: Would it not just be easier to measure the distance using the scale of the map? The obvious answer to that question is yes. However, I used this practice a number of times when discovering property lines and gas pipelines in wilderness environments. Often, my team and I had maps that had been hand drawn 100 years or more before our surveys. We would often navigate utilizing these hand drawn maps and a compass to find all the property-line markers and iron pins.

USING TRIANGLES AND SQUARES TO NAVIGATE

Another way to utilize our eighth-grade education is to understand how to utilize a triangle, square and circle to go into a wilderness environment using only your compass and your pace count. In school, you may recall that an equilateral triangle is one in which all three sides have the same length and each angle is 60 degrees. It is rather easy to rely on this information to go into an unknown area, even without trails, and navigate in and out safely (see image 74). I use this method regularly when doing wildlife or nature studies. It allows me to randomly go into an unknown area, look for wildlife or specific

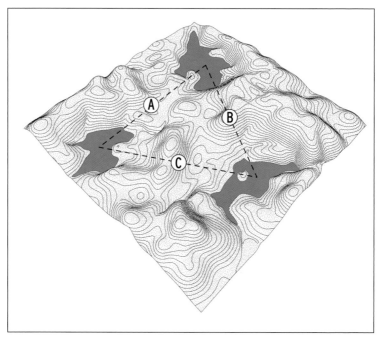

Image 74: An equilateral triangle on a map will help you cover an area that approximates a triangular shape.

plant species and return. This is especially true when documenting wildlife nesting structures or similar. Use of these shapes to navigate also permits first responders to go into an area and navigate efficiently for fugitive apprehension or lost-person rescue.

You can see this on a large scale or a small one. You can see how easy this would be with a triangle (see image 74), or you could do a box search and follow the sizing of a square or rectangle as well. A quick glance at a map or the environment in front of you will tell you which geometric figure fits your overall need in your current circumstance.

A similar exercise with one slight adjustment can be undertaken to do a box search of the area. Start off with a square but shorten the lengths of the sides as you get close to intersecting lines of the square (see image 75). This is a simple yet valuable method when you are searching in a wilderness.

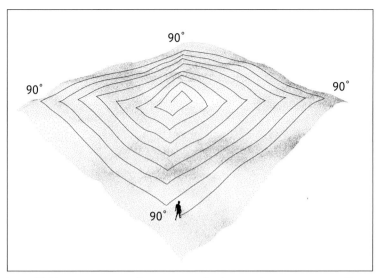

Image 75: Use your compass and pace count to do a box search to cover an area well.

Some examples of this include the following scenarios:

- Search-and-rescue workers will use this method when covering a specific area to find a lost person.

- Trackers will sometimes use this or similar methods to find an initial sign or lost sign of the quarry they are tracking.

- Wildlife biologists can use this method to locate nesting areas for wildlife.

- Plant biologists can utilize this method to map out an area in a wilderness and document all or specific species in an area of study.

- Anyone can utilize this method if they have lost something in a general area. This method will force you to limit the area you are searching directly in front of you and will at the same time cover the area so nothing is missed.

USING A TRIANGLE TO DETERMINE THE SLOPE

We are quite sure you spent a fair amount of time in school developing X-Y axes for many projects. Whether it be economics, recipes or biology, utilizing an X-Y axis to give a visual reference to subject matter makes it more understandable. One of the most common things new wilderness navigators have difficulty with is understanding a slope based on the contour lines. One way that we can improve our understanding is to draw a triangle that depicts the distance traveled on the X axis and the change in elevation on the Y axis. In image 76, you can see a triangle that represents a gently sloping hike. This also depicts a hike with a drastic elevation change.

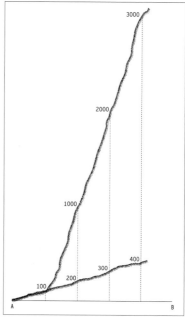

Image 76: Plotting out your slope and recognizing a steep or gradual climb is valuable information for planning.

By doing a few of these graphs, you should be able to see these elevation changes better. If you also go and hike these locations, you can equate the elevation change of the triangle to how you actually feel while walking it.

LEARN BY DOING

We realize there is a lot of technical information in this chapter, which may make your learning process feel intimidating. That's why it's important you learn by doing—do the math while you're actually outdoors practicing. Experiential learning is the most valuable piece of wilderness navigation. It is the reason this book is the size and shape it is: so that it is easy to take on the trail with you.

USING A CIRCLE

A simple exercise that can be completed by using a circle will require you to be able to judge distances. Please reference chapter 4 for the section on judging distances in the field (page 114). In this instance, you should consider a central point that you can locate on a map or in the field. Imagine that you are tied to that central point by a rope of a certain distance and walk a circle around it (see image 77). This works best in an area where you do not lose sight of the

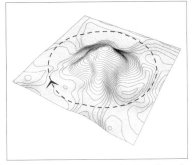

Image 77: Use a well-defined and easily recognized feature to do a quick circular search of an area.

feature that is your central point. I have completed this exercise by using a fire tower, a very tall rock outcropping and a cell tower at different times.

Now that you have read all of that, please take the time to go ahead and contact that eighth-grade teacher and say thank you. You blew through that stuff just to pass a test back in the day. You had no idea you would be using it to navigate in the wilderness. Enjoy your memories of geometry class!

QUESTIONS FOR PRACTICE

There are only 3 questions here in this practice section, but they are doozies. They put together a lot of the things you have learned thus far. I am sure you can do it, though.

1. There is a benchmark at these coordinates on the map enclosed with this book: 17S 279836 4217657. Imagine yourself standing at that point. You look north and see two hilltops. You note on your map that these are referred to as Twin Knobs. Find the angles and distance from your position to those two hilltops.

2. Let's assume you have gone hiking and are exploring Trough Lick Branch Hollow, which is on the enclosed map. You find a spot that has some artifacts on it that you would like to report to the United States Forest Service. You do not have a GPS, but you can see Tater Knob hilltop from your location. You use your compass from your position and determine Tater Knob hilltop is 159 degrees magnetic from your position. What are your coordinates at that location? Hints: You will want to use a back azimuth from Tater Knob tower and draw the appropriate line. If you don't have a map tool to get it exactly, go ahead and order yourself one now. You can still make an estimate using just the grid lines shown on the map. Also, don't forget that your compass reading is magnetic, not map, so you will need to adjust for declination.

3. Let's assume that I've gone squirrel hunting down the hollow that follows Buck Creek indicated on your map. I find a big opening about 1¼ miles (2 km) into the hunt. At this opening, I find a place that I think had an old homesite, because next to the forest opening I see several fruit trees and some American chestnut trees, all of which are still producing fruit and nuts. Process that in your mind and then list some of the wilderness navigation methods you could use to find those trees.

Answers: (1) The western hilltop is 360 degrees and 528 feet (161 m) away. The eastern hilltop is 15 degrees and 541 feet (165 m). (2) You should have come up with something close to these coordinates: 17S 275695 4217341. (3) Park at the head of Buck Creek Hollow, walk to the approximate location and create a rectangle search area when you get there. Keep your situational awareness on as you search and find your trees.

AMERICAN CHESTNUT TREES

The story related in question 3 from "Questions for Practice" (page 206) is completely true and the answer given is exactly what I did to find the trees my uncle told me about. A leaf from one of those American chestnut trees appears as a drawing my wife created for the Nature Reliance School logo you can see on the dedication page. (If you are not familiar with why live American chestnut trees are an important discovery, look them up. It is an interesting study on nature awareness and our forests.) I tell you all this because wilderness navigation is a fun and important practice that can lead to interesting discoveries.

SPECIALIZED PRACTICAL APPLICATIONS OF WILDERNESS NAVIGATION METHODS

You have heard me talk about building the wilderness navigation puzzle throughout this book. At this point, that puzzle has been placed together. After looking at it, you notice it would look even better with a nice border around it. That metaphorical border is what I will be covering in the following chapters. Tracy and I have taught a wide range of people who utilize wilderness navigation. Search-and-rescue teams, tactical personnel and families and youth (especially scouts) are all groups that need some dedicated help. While we wrote this section with those individuals in mind, the advice in the following pages is not just for those groups—anyone can learn valuable skills in these chapters; however, if you are part of one of these specialized groups, this section will resonate with you and your work.

CHAPTER 9

WILDERNESS NAVIGATION FOR SEARCH AND RESCUE

Walking is man's best medicine. —Hippocrates

As you have seen throughout this book, many of these opening stories happened in the distant past. The one we are sharing with you now happened the night before this chapter was written and deserves to be told.

At approximately 10:00 p.m. on a hot summer night, an area search-and-rescue team received a call from 911 dispatch stating that they had received a phone call from two lost hikers in the Red River Gorge. The team that received the initial call was able to make phone contact with the lost hikers. The incident was then passed on to a different search-and-rescue team, of which Tracy is a member.

One way that Tracy and other SAR personnel like him add value to their teams is through regularly traveling the areas they operate in. Having this level of familiarity allows them to be highly knowledgeable about the topography and features of the areas they are responsible for. Tracy also made short contact with the lost hikers before cell phone reception was lost. He was able to discern their general location before they were cut off; however, without an exact location, Tracy determined the best course of action would be to involve other search-and-rescue teams so they could provide mutual aid. There were three different entry points into which teams could access the area. This sort of information was discerned in two ways. The first is that Tracy and the other SAR team members had extensive experience in the area. The second is that many SAR personnel first develop an understanding of an area by utilizing a map. Had this particular incident happened in an area the searchers were not familiar with, either a physical map or mapping app would have been an invaluable resource in developing a plan of rescue.

Once the SAR teams entered the wilderness, one of the teams came upon the hikers approximately 1½ miles (2 km) into the area. The searchers discovered that one of the hikers had an injured ankle and could not walk the entire way *out to their vehicle. Another team came in with a Stokes basket to carry the injured hiker out of the area. Once again, because the searchers had extensive experience of the area from both their own travels and their use of maps and mapping software, they knew the most productive path into and out of the area with the Stokes basket. As with many search-and-rescue operations, intimate knowledge of the area derived by solid wilderness navigation skills was the key to getting these hikers safely out and on their way home.*

The purpose of this chapter is twofold. We want to introduce you to some of the methods that search-and-rescue personnel utilize to find lost persons. This will include some methods above and beyond wilderness navigation. This is different than the methods we shared in chapter 5. The methods in that chapter were ways to increase your chances of being found if you are ever a lost hiker. In this chapter, our goal is to get you in the mind-set of a searcher, which will serve to increase your wilderness navigation skill set. Secondly, we want to assist our readers who are involved in active and regular search-and-rescue operations in developing their wilderness navigation skill set.

EMERGENCY MIND-SET

SAR personnel need to be able to perform under pressure. This includes utilizing your wilderness navigation skill set to find others in the first place and then to get those people extracted safely and efficiently. This is especially true when the individuals you are rescuing have a serious injury. As we have mentioned many times throughout this text, we have a wonderful opportunity to train with some incredibly well-qualified personnel who do their jobs under heaping amounts of pressure. Explosive Ordnance Disposal (EOD) personnel are some of these people. These are the specialists the military and law enforcement agencies call to handle explosive devices. One mistake by these individuals and many people are likely to get hurt (including the EOD specialists). Their thoughts on how to stay calm under pressure are good for any of us and apply directly to both SAR personnel and someone who is lost. By remaining calm, you can utilize wilderness navigation skills to accomplish one of two actions:

- Find your location with certainty so you can begin a self-rescue operation.

- Recognize that you do not have the ability to do wilderness navigation at any point and put into action fundamental survival skills we discussed in chapter 5.

One training opportunity afforded to us with EOD personnel offered the following three methods of putting you in the best mind-set possible to make hard decisions under the stress of a search-and-rescue event.

ASSESS THE PROBLEMS AND THREATS, AND PRIORITIZE THE SEARCH BASED ON THE MOST LIKELY

Safety and survival require you to objectively look at the situation and best determine what the problem is. As it relates to wilderness navigation and SAR operations, this means you must consider the direction, terrain and people involved (i.e., the people you are working with and the people in need of rescue). If you spread out the map and see that you may need ropes for a high-angle rescue or that you may need a carry basket because the patient cannot walk out on their own, you are assessing what the problems are by using your map skills. The decision to either have those items on standby with another team that is ready to assist or to take the equipment with you will depend on an in-person assessment by a team leader on the scene. The team leader can utilize their knowledge of the area, the available maps and the available personnel to call in others for mutual aid or to go at it immediately.

It is vital to understand that most searches should *start* on the map. Trails, terrain and waterways can all be evaluated by looking at the map. This evaluation will then lead to an efficient plan of action that can be shared with all teams before they head out on their searches. Searching should always include map knowledge. It does not consist of just walking a trail or using your GPS to navigate to and from waypoints.

FOCUS ON THE THINGS YOU CAN CONTROL, NOT ON THE THINGS YOU CANNOT

In any given SAR operation, you typically do not get the opportunity to determine the time or the place that you will be needed. You can, however, get as much experience as you can in an area by studying it with maps and software. This is a necessity for teams that work the large national parks or open areas such as Yosemite National Park, which by itself covers 761,266 acres (3,080 sq. km). It is humanly impossible for a single search-and-rescue person to know that land by walking it and reviewing it. Flyovers in aircraft should be undertaken whenever possible. In addition to flyovers, take the free opportunities you have to review your maps of the area. Seek out senior team leaders and those with more experience so you can familiarize yourself with the areas in which someone could get lost. At the same time, know that you cannot control where people end up when they need rescuing. Be ready to enter an area where no one has ever completed a rescue. You should be mentally prepared for the timing to be terrible and the weather to be the same. Again, those are things you cannot control— you should focus on things you *can* control instead.

STUDY AND TRAIN TO KNOW WHAT THE NEXT STEP SHOULD BE

Anyone who works under pressure can tell you that decision-making is minimized under high-stress conditions. Professionals who work under pressure recognize this and do what they can to develop an orderly method of handling such situations. That does not mean they do not have contingencies prepared if or when something unexpected occurs. Rather, they have a process to follow that assists in unplanned events. For example, it would be a worthwhile investment of time to use maps to determine the best way to go into and out of an area you may regularly visit. Have an exit plan in place before you go. This way, if you make contact with a lost or injured person 10 miles (16 km) into a mountainous valley in Yosemite, you'll know the best option for extract is a helicopter. On the other hand, if they are only 2 miles (3 km) into the wilderness, you may be able to get the work completed with an all-terrain vehicle. Having plans in place before you need them is invaluable.

To effectively plan ahead for wilderness navigation operations, it's helpful to be familiar with SAR methodologies. There are essentially four types of search techniques utilized by trained SAR personnel:

- **Theoretical search:** This involves determining the LKP or LPS and developing a search based on that information. By knowing how long a person has been lost and how far they can walk in that time frame, the team can then focus the search area involved.

- **Statistical search:** This search technique uses previous data known from lost persons to limit the search area even more so than the preceding method. The primary data used is the lost person's age, distance traveled, likely travel areas, mental state and medication needs, among other details. These pieces of data help establish the area the lost person is most likely to be in.

- **Deductive reasoning:** This is used when a search team limits or expands a search area based on knowledge of the lost individual. As an example, this could include knowing the lost person was hiking to a spot to photograph something in particular, knowing they had taken fishing gear with them or knowing they were wanting to find wildflowers for naturalist studies. These bits of information allow the searchers to go to an area of interest specific to the lost person and search for them.

- **Combination:** This is the method used by most teams. By utilizing a combination of the preceding methods, SAR teams can uncover more wilderness navigation puzzle pieces. The more puzzle pieces you can put together, the more efficient the search is.

Now that we have built a fundamental search mind-set and skill set, let's consider some specific searching techniques. We will specifically look at how to implement wilderness navigation methods along with them.

HASTY SEARCH

A hasty search is one in which SAR teams are sent into an area that is likely to contain the lost person they seek. Often this starts at the LKP and extends out in the direction of the place the person was likely going. It is a search that travels quickly to likely spots, such as a barn or a popular swimming hole. It may also be employed to rapidly clear a popular camping site or a gravel access road. In short, hasty searches are used to clear obvious or likely areas in a minimal amount of time.

Following are some guidelines for hasty searches:

- Hasty teams should consist of at least one pair going out do the search. Going solo, you increase the likelihood of a searcher also getting lost or injured. Sending teams out in pairs ensures there are two team members who can combine their knowledge on the topography and consult each other with a map.

- Since hasty teams are typically moving out in directions away from a single starting point, it is easy to give each team an azimuth to go out on. The team leader can determine these azimuths in such a way that an equal "slice of pie" can be searched by each pair of searchers.

- Terrain will always dictate movement patterns. If team members encounter an obstacle during the search, they can navigate with compasses around the obstacle and get back on their heading once they maneuver around it. In rough terrain this means that rather than the commander delegating certain sections of a pie, the searchers will likely be sent to the areas of travel (such as hollows, streams and ridgelines).

- When communicating with incident command or other team members, it is best to communicate in terms of cardinal direction rather than left or right. In heavy vegetation or other terrain where it is difficult to communicate, referring to cardinal directions will help other members know where their teammates are located (e.g., "I am currently northeast of the trail that was leaving the LKP").

- All team leaders and team members should review the details in chapter 1 about contour lines and how to utilize them. When SAR team members are sent into the wilderness, understanding contour lines will give immediate feedback as to where likely avenues of travel are located. Team leaders can also more effectively offer the searchers the ability to know what should be avoided. Cliff lines or steep terrain are perfect examples of this.

The hope of this hasty search is to bring the search to a quick end. The longer a search continues, the more opportunities arise for the lost person to become injured or worse.

SWEEP SEARCH

A sweep search is exactly what it sounds like: an effort on the part of a search team to "sweep" through an area much like a broom sweeping up particles on the floor. The searchers spread out on a line, then they all travel in the same direction in parallel lines. The distance between searchers is dictated by the terrain. This means they will have enough distance between one another that they can make visual contact with one another and still effectively scan the area. This type of search is most often used in areas containing level ground. Hilly or mountainous areas are not suitable for this type of search. Wilderness navigation skills can also be utilized effectively here:

- The team leader is given the direction, azimuth and distance, and they then direct their team members. This includes the leader keeping the searchers on the same line and within a distance such that the terrain can be adequately searched. By staying on one line, the searchers can efficiently sweep the area.

- The team leader being responsible for directing the team allows each member to focus their attention on searching. If the individual team members are responsible for the azimuth, direction and distance, their attention is diverted.

SQUARE SEARCH

A square search is another search technique that is best employed in a fairly level area. In a square search, a team of searchers perform an ever-widening search that radiates on straight lines from the LKP. This type of search can be completed with a good grasp of pace or time count and a compass, as the following instructions reveal:

- Choose a direction from the LKP and walk in one directional heading (such as north).

- You can choose to walk with the pace count method by walking out a predetermined number of paces. You can alternatively walk out for a predetermined amount of time.

- Once that distance or time is reached, use your compass to turn 90 degrees and walk another straight-line distance that is longer than the original line.

- Continue following the preceding steps until you have created a square spiral of the area. The distance or time chosen will be dictated by the terrain and vegetation. If you cannot see very far, the spiral will be shorter.

Please note that on a large scale, the preceding instructions can also be employed by aircraft. Pilots can do an ever-widening search from the LKP to effectively cover an area on the ground or at sea.

CHOKE-POINT SEARCH

A choke-point search is best utilized by a larger team that has the manpower to put a smaller team out and away from the others. Choke points are locations within a large area that contains natural or man-made features that force foot traffic to be funneled into a much smaller area. These could include a saddle crossing between two ridges, the area between two steep cliff lines (such as a gorge) or a man-made or natural bridge that is the easiest means of crossing a waterway. Wilderness navigation skills can assist in choke-point searches in the following ways:

- SAR teams will need to study the map to see the choke points that are in the direction of travel of the lost person.

- SAR team leaders must gather coordinates from those areas and distribute them among the team members. A team leader will assign smaller teams to go to the choke points and watch for the lost person.

- Along the way to the choke points, SAR personnel may find clues that they can then radio back to incident command. Each person must have wilderness navigation skills with a protractor and map or the use of GPS to get those coordinates accurately.

CONTAINMENT SEARCH

A containment search is one in which search teams are placed on the outermost perimeter of the search area. This essentially stops the hiker from continuing to walk from the search area and creates a boundary for the search. This type of search should be completed by those who have lots of energy and the ability to visually search and call to the lost hiker while moving at a steady pace. A containment search will most likely comprise many miles of walking. It will be necessary for the containment search teams to communicate effectively on their location. This will require an understanding of the terrain and adequate knowledge of topography or GPS devices to report this information.

TRACK-TRAP SEARCH

A track-trap search is similar to a choke-point search in that teams determine where, using maps or thorough knowledge of the area, searchers are most likely to pick up tracks. Areas that contain sandy, muddy or snowy ground are places that will easily take and hold tracks. If these areas are known, team members can again be assigned to go directly to them to investigate and see if any tracks have been made there. The individual members must have adequate training in mantracking to be able to ascertain what or who made the tracks if they find them. (See the sidebar for the fundamentals of tracking on page 220.)

Search-and-rescue operations and wilderness navigation skills go together like peanut butter and jelly. Where does one end and the other begin? That is a difficult question to answer, and for good reason. They *should* be inseparable. In all emergency-response training, including medicine, search and rescue or even law enforcement, one of the first items taught is that responders are number one. This may seem selfish and uncaring at first, but that cannot be further from the truth. These are the types of people that you, I and our fellow citizens call on when we need help. They must think of themselves as number one for the sole purpose of sizing up a situation and not become a statistic. If a search-and-rescue person goes into a wilderness without adequate wilderness navigation training, they, too, could become lost. If that were to happen, the SAR team would then have a compounding problem: more people lost and fewer searchers to search. That math does not add up well for the search.

FUNDAMENTALS OF TRACKING

Tracy and I are heavily involved in the practice and use of tracking as a tool to find a quarry. That quarry might be a lost person or fugitive or a deer during hunting season. Tracking is a lifelong endeavor, and time spent practicing it is never wasted. We want to offer you some tracking fundamentals here to help you on your next search.

The term sign, as it relates to tracking, encompasses the indicators that reveal something or someone has passed by an area. We discussed the concept of baseline versus disturbance in chapter 5. There are three primary types of sign to consider here. (Please note this is not an exhaustive listing as we are giving you only five examples of each; there are many more.)

1. Ground sign is any sign that appears on the ground below the height of your ankle. Some examples include the following:

- Tracks or partial tracks left on the earth.
- Bruised, bent or broken vegetation.
- Creases in leaves.
- Overturned leaves.
- Transfer of one medium to another (e.g., water splashed from a creek onto the bank).

2. Aerial sign is sign that is found above the level of the ankle. Some examples include the following:

- Tall blades of grass intertwined, often referred to as pointers because they point in the direction of travel.
- Broken branches.
- Disturbed cobwebs (note that this can be deceiving, because spiders can build webs in just a few minutes under the right conditions).
- Bark missing from a tree due to hand placement, hammock straps or a person looking for fire material.
- Rain or dew missing from leaves because someone brushed up against it.

3. Intangible sign is sign that falls outside of these categories and is often lumped in with miscellaneous sign:

- Saliva, urine or feces left behind.

- Odors from a person or fire.

- Sounds unnatural to the environment, such as pots clanging, zippers moving or hook-and-loop closures unlatching.

- Animal alarm sounds, such as deer snorting or wheezing, birds chattering excitedly or insects stirring.

- Garbage left behind, such as food-storage bags, tobacco by-products or similar man-made items.

To prevent tragedy, we hope all searchers take time to study and practice the methods discussed in the preceding sections to better navigate their way into and out of a wilderness area. The whole reason the searchers are dedicated to this task? "That others may live."

WILDERNESS NAVIGATION WITH OTHER SEARCHERS

In any search-and-rescue mission, working efficiently and effectively with others is a key component to success. Here are several points related to wilderness navigation that SAR teams must consider:

- First and foremost, a search should utilize an accurate topography map at incident command. When commanders brief the searchers on team responsibilities, there should be many open-ended questions to team leaders to verify that each team understands their area of responsibility. Close-ended questions that only receive yes or no answers are not adequate. People will inherently answer in the way they think they are supposed to answer. For example, don't ask a question such as, "Team Leader 1, do you understand the area that I want you to search?" Rather, ask a question such as, "Team Leader 1, please tell me or show me on the map the areas I want you to search." Commanders can then get credible feedback that the entire area of possibility is being searched.

- When communicating coordinates via radio to other team members or incident command, verify that those receiving the coordinates received them correctly by repeating them. In general, it is best to give the easting coordinates and ask for a repeat, then ask for the northing coordinates and ask for a repeat. When you ask, "How copy?" the receiver should repeat all the coordinates back with another break between easting and northing numbers.

- Many apps allow you to send waypoints of importance to anyone that has cell coverage. Ensure when you do this that you provide as much information as you can. Do not assume that anyone receiving them understands your intent. Nearly all GPS units that can download the data and cell phone GPS units have areas for notes. This information is definitely one of those things that is better to have and not need than to need and not have.

- Incident command and search teams should expect that communication issues will arise during every search. If you have several searchers out and those searchers are dependent on radios or cell phones to relay important information, you should have contingency plans in place. In addition, as you send teams out there should be a window of time designated for searchers to be back. If they do not meet that window, then others should search for them as well. Viewing the map and having primary, secondary and tertiary methods for communicating the safety of the team should cover most issues.

Image 78: Open communication with others is key to being an effective team doing wilderness navigation.

QUESTIONS FOR PRACTICE

1. Understanding and preplanning SAR events in a given area helps with what?

2. One of the most critical things you can do as a lost person is to what?

3. It is difficult for our minds to be attentive to things of importance when we are under stress. What things should we focus on for search-and-rescue operations?

4. The area identified using topo features on a map where a lost hiker must hike through is known as what?

5. An area that might capture a lost person's boot print is known as what?

6. How can an SAR team utilize wilderness navigation during a hasty search?

7. In a containment search, is it necessary for the search teams to have wilderness navigation skills, since they are moving so quickly and on the outer boundary of the search area?

8. If a lost hiker texts or calls 911 and tells the dispatcher that their coordinates are 34°47'83" N by -83°46'48" W, does a searcher have enough information to locate them?

9. If you were tracking someone in an area and noticed that their step length increased dramatically, what would that tell you?

Answers: (1) Making decisions during a stressful event. (2) Stop where you are and remain calm. (3) The things we can control. (4) A choke point. (5) A track trap. (6) By giving an azimuth to the teams and having them investigate those areas. (7) Yes. They will need to report to incident command their position and any clues they find. Although they are on the outer boundary, new information from them or other teams may necessitate changing their original plan and navigating to another area quickly. Wilderness navigation skills are necessary to do this safely. (8) No. The information given cannot be accurate, because Lat/Long seconds cannot be more than 60. Therefore, the 34°47'83" cannot be correct. (9) That they began running.

SHELTOWEE TRACE

NATIONAL RECREATION TRAIL

COLE GRAPHIC SOLUTIONS
877-994-6600

C-09018

CHAPTER 10

NAVIGATING WHILE ARMED FOR HUNTING OR LAW ENFORCEMENT

To hunt successfully, you must know your ground, your pack and your quarry.
—*K.J. Parker*

My abilities as a tracker and navigator have been used on a few occasions to assist area law-enforcement officers in forensic follow-ups. These are situations in which there is a high probability that the individual being looked for is deceased, and it is the job of the searcher to go to the areas and aid any other assets available in locating a body. Preservation of evidence is key. In situations like this, it is important to have an incident command with strong control over the scene so that it is not contaminated by the searchers to the point that there is no longer any usable evidence when the body is found.

I was part of a forensic search on a private farm in a nearby county. Law-enforcement searchers and canines had been employed for two days and a Black Hawk helicopter had also been utilized. The farm was also home to several cows, so disturbance in the area was a certainty. It was my job as a tracker to help distinguish between human sign and cattle sign. Tracking was difficult in the tall grass and other sign present.

The first order of business for me was to review the search map with incident command and determine what had and had not been searched.

Understanding a topography map was imperative to the search. I also needed to report back to incident command with the coordinates of the box searches that I completed in an effort to find sign and other indicators of human movement patterns, especially those that indicated someone moving a body.

After coming up with nothing more than a lot of cattle tracks, I was tasked to go to areas that had already been searched and utilize tracking methods to search for sign. Again, I started by getting the coordinates of the boxes already searched. I systematically went through each area, navigating with GPS to cover *each box before moving on. As darkness was descending and the search was coming to a stop, I was searching an area and saw some lumber that had been recently moved. I noticed this because I had painstakingly looked over every meter of each box. Canine cadaver units had already searched the area, so this locale had been marked off as searched. It was the simple former farm boy as well as the skilled navigator and tracker within me that recognized the lumber had been displaced.*

I notified incident command of this situation. The huge pile of lumber was moved and the canines were brought in again. This time they hit the area where the lumber had been before the law-enforcement officers moved it as they painstakingly looked for other evidence along the way. The displaced lumber was hiding a shallow grave containing the body, which had been wrapped in several layers of plastic, covered up with soil and then covered with the lumber.

The systematic tandem use of navigation and tracking helped the law-enforcement officers close in on their investigation.

At Nature Reliance School, we consider it a great pleasure to train a broad range of students in our backcountry skills courses. One segment of our student base includes those who carry firearms while doing backcountry skills. We have trained a wide range of law-enforcement officers on the federal, state and local levels. We have also trained many hunters. Our law-enforcement friends utilize wilderness navigation as they serve in one of two capacities: (1) during mantracking and fugitive apprehension, or (2) in search-and-rescue related events. In this chapter, we want to share some specific information for these groups.

It is important to consider the principles discussed in this chapter on their own because an individual hiker, or even a group of hikers, without weapons affect only those in their immediate vicinity. Law-enforcement personnel and hunters carry firearms that will reach much farther. Wilderness navigation helps these individuals be safer in remote areas. Safety is vital in all wilderness activities, but probably more so when carrying and possibly discharging a firearm into the area. Review the four primary rules of gun safety in the sidebar.

JEFF COOPER'S FOUR RULES OF GUN SAFETY

1. Treat all guns as if they are loaded.
2. Never point a gun at anything you are not willing to destroy.
3. Keep your finger off the trigger until your sights are on the target and you have made the decision to shoot.
4. Be sure of your target and what lies beyond it.

The four rules of gun safety listed in the sidebar have been around for quite some time. And for good reason—they encompass a lot of important information. Since firearms have an added layer of danger if not used properly, it is worth a wilderness navigator's effort to study the terrain and make assessments based on it before ever going afield. Terrain analysis is a term typically utilized by military personnel. It is a way by which they can prepare or understand a battlefield area. We are going to use some common military terrain analysis procedures here for use in law enforcement and hunting. Wilderness navigation plays a significant role in all terrain analysis procedures.

There are three main categories of terrain analysis as it relates to our usage here:

- **Template analysis:** This involves looking at a map and determining in which areas our quarry is most likely located.

- **Maneuver analysis:** This analysis will dictate the ways we move into and out of an area. The goal of maneuver analysis is preparing for the breach analysis.

- **Breach analysis:** This involves the planning that goes into executing the hunt for the quarry and includes equipment needed to complete the task. We should be able to make contact with the quarry, not be surprised before reaching them, and complete the task.

WILDERNESS NAVIGATION FOR HUNTING PURPOSES

Let us put the preceding terrain analyses to work on a simulated white-tailed deer hunt. Please review image 79.

If this is the area that you have access to for a hunt, you should take a walk through the area and start gathering data about it. You do not need to walk every portion of the land to study it. You can find a high elevation and use binoculars to get a better understanding of the land. You can also do this by only looking at the map; however, if you only use the map, there are a few items that you need to be prepared to deal with when you go into the area for the hunt:

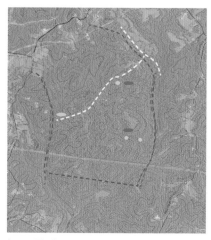

Image 79: A map is a great resource for pre- and postplanning of hunting trips.

- Topography maps do not detail the density of the vegetation for any given area. Only foot travel will allow you to determine this. What if an area has been recently logged? That will drastically change the patterns of all wildlife.

- Topography maps do not share the types of vegetation growing in an area. An area might look like it holds wildlife, but that area might also have only pine trees growing in it. White-tailed deer are more likely to be in hardwood areas than pines.

- There are several areas of likely travel. A good tracker can go into these areas and determine which ones are the most heavily used.

- There will always be prevailing wind patterns, but in hilly rather than mountainous areas, winds will be directed by the hills in different ways. Being on the ground will allow you to see leaf pileups behind trees and the crescent shapes of dirt, snow or leaves that we mentioned in chapter 7.

In the modern world, few people have significant time to invest in hunting, but providing your own food source is an incredibly rewarding experience. With time constraints as they are, utilizing terrain analysis for hunting purposes will save us some time afield. In the list on page 38, we presented problems that could occur by using only the map; however, the map does allow us the opportunity to gather important information before we ever go there. Now let's talk about how we can use terrain analysis and this map to accomplish our goals.

TEMPLATE ANALYSIS

Template analysis is looking at a map and determining in which areas our quarry is most likely located.

Template analysis includes your ability to take known information—such as wildlife patterns, food and water sources and areas of safety for bedding—and apply them to the map. Some of these you will be able to discern with the topography map; others will be dictated by the vegetation and other natural resources in the area, which can only be discovered on foot. Following are some recommendations you can implement when doing a template analysis for our hunting example:

- Mark areas that are likely travel corridors for white-tailed deer. These areas are removed from common human activity—travel corridors.

- Mark areas that are likely areas for daybeds for deer. Deer are mostly nocturnal and will lie down during the day. They tend to do this in areas where they have easy escape routes in multiple directions.

- Mark likely feeding areas. White-tailed deer like "edge habitat" where a forest meets an open area. These are the areas deer will likely travel to when they get out of their daybeds.

- Mark likely areas for water. White-tailed deer will travel to water each day at minimum, often more than once.

- Mark what you believe to be the best area to set up a deer stand or blind or to start a hunt at daylight.

MANEUVER ANALYSIS

Maneuver analysis will dictate the ways we move into and out of an area. The goal of maneuver analysis is preparing for the breach analysis.

For our scenario, let's assume we want to camp in the area for a three-day hunt. We will need to consider ways to get to these areas that will make the least impact on the deer's normal activity. Here are some considerations for this analysis:

- Deer will be used to human activity near the roads leading to this area. Therefore, a campsite that is close to the road will be optimal. I have marked a primary and secondary area for camping that takes that into consideration.

- We must consider being out of sight of passersby when we leave camp. Depending on the area that we hunt, we may need to avoid opportunistic thieves. If we must leave some items in camp, we want them to be there when we get back.

BREACH ANALYSIS

Let's assume we have accomplished our task of taking a deer. Now what? In this example, it is legal and ethical to utilize a vehicle to pick up our deer. We can easily come to the location of the deer and pick it up with a truck or all-terrain vehicle. Here are some considerations for doing so:

- We can examine the roads into the area to see if it will require a vehicle with a winch, four-wheel drive or similar features. This is a small area, and it's easy to decipher this need. However, quarry retrieval can be complicated by a backcountry harvest of an elk or similar animal. In that situation, we may have to hike in several miles. Having access to haul it out is imperative to getting our meat out safely.

- If we did happen to be deep in a backcountry area, especially in the West, Northeast and Northwest, vehicle travel may be illegal. We could arrive on horseback to get the meat out. This will require adequate water sources at least for the horse. If the portage out requires multiday travel, we will also need to consider taking food or finding grazing areas along the way. A map can offer insight into this as well.

- If we need to literally drag the deer out, understanding the elevation changes will important. Taking a straight-line distance from the stand area to the vehicle is possible but will be very hard work. By noting the various inroads we can more easily find a better route out.

FINAL THOUGHTS ON NAVIGATING THE WILDERNESS WHILE HUNTING

Each of the preceding sections detail ways to assist you in looking at one specific area for a deer hunt. But what about other types of hunting, such as elk hunting, where you will likely travel several miles to find your quarry? Or grouse or pheasant hunting, in which you travel wide ranges of open ground to flush birds? Wilderness navigation can be used in all of these situations. Let's consider a few possible scenarios:

- When hunting large game, you will need to cover two aspects of the hunt that wilderness navigation skills can assist with. The first is obvious: how to get to the hunting area and how to hunt it, which we have shown here. Second, you must also plan accordingly for when game is harvested and you must get it out in a timely manner. For many years, I hunted white-tailed deer in a spot in which I had to drag the deer up a very steep incline after harvest. I noticed several years later that a small access road was visible below the area I was hunting. If I had consulted a map I would have known this. After making this discovery, I began easily dragging my harvested deer down the hill rather than up.

- Using a GPS tracker is a great way to work an area in which you hope to flush birds for hunting. If you set your GPS to track your steps, or if it utilizes a "breadcrumbs" feature, you will get a visual on the areas you have already hunted. This allows you to more systematically cover ground in an effort to flush birds for harvest.

- In my Gaia app, I now record locations in which I find deer sign on the areas that I hunt. I spend lots of time there (it's where I do most of my writing, as well as where I film my YouTube videos and conduct research). By doing this on in the Gaia app, I can save layers that contain only deer sign and then pull the data up and look at it online. This gives me a quick visual reference to regular patterns of deer travel.

- In the unfortunate event that you need to track a large game animal that is shot poorly and you know it will travel far, you can use your map or GPS to save all areas where you find blood or other sign along the way. By doing this, you can more readily see the direction the animal is heading. Since most animals will head to cover, you can then use your map to locate the likely sources of cover. If you lose the sign and need to find it, you will likely find it along the same line heading to cover. The common tracking term is "cutting for sign"—this is a procedure by which you go to areas that likely contain sign and search for it. (Do not spend too much time in areas where it is hard to discern tracks and other sign.)

WILDERNESS NAVIGATION FOR MILITARY OR LAW-ENFORCEMENT PURPOSES

Sometimes developing old-fashioned skills and coupling them with modern technology is the way for those in the modern tactical community to assist in fugitive apprehension, insurgent apprehension and forensic follow-ups (as discussed in our opening story for this chapter). We have trained personnel from several agencies in backcountry wilderness skills. Those personnel have regularly employed those skills in the line of duty. There are several key points that all law enforcement should be aware of when learning land navigation for their work:

- Understanding grid systems and which system each agency you interact with uses is an absolute must. Administration should make every attempt to synchronize the grid system being used across agencies. This includes agencies on the federal, state and local levels, as well as aircraft units. Many aircraft can convert coordinates at the push of a button. This is good to know, because ground units may be in pursuit or in search of armed individuals—not the time to be concerned about converting coordinates. Let those in incident command or the aircraft do the converting. They are away from the action. But again, this risky situation can be mitigated if each team utilizes the same coordinate system.

- Terrain analysis is imperative to any sort of active search for dangerous individuals. All fatal funnels and other advantageous positions for the quarry should be considered at incident command via consulting a map. If a team is mantracking toward a quarry that is heading to high ground, tactical decision-making will need to be adjusted to contain the individual.

- Incident command has the "big picture" of this sort of operation. Their intelligence analysts will have the training to assimilate the information and relay important information back to the teams in the field. When relaying coordinates to incident command, verify that you are correct before getting on the radio to send information to the commanders.

In the US military, what we have been referring to as wilderness navigation in this book is most often referred to as land navigation. The military does a good job of training its personnel in land navigation, but even that entity has become increasingly dependent on technology for many practices—including land navigation. Due to this fact, companies such as Nature Reliance School will train military personnel who come to us wanting to refresh skills they have already learned or pick up an extra "trick" or two to give them an advantage in other schools and training courses. This is especially true for those who are interested in schools such as Special Forces Assessment and Selection or similar training.

FUNDAMENTALS FOR SPECIAL FORCES ASSESSMENT AND SELECTION AND OTHER RELATED TRAINING COURSES

We have a great friend who has a background in Special Forces Assessment and Selection. We queried him on how we can best serve personnel seeking that sort of training and understanding. He gave us an outline of how we can best serve your needs in that arena as well:

- Know how to orient your map so that it matches the terrain in front of you (we covered this in chapter 1).

- Know how to locate yourself on the map. You can do this by terrain association (consult chapter 1) or GPS (consult chapter 3). This is a vital step, so it is worth your effort in double-checking to verify. Once you are certain you have located your position on the map, make sure you write the coordinates down. Unless otherwise noted, all military maps will be in MGRS (for more about grid systems, see page 78).

- Depending on the course requirements, you will most likely need to navigate to a certain point. This will require you to plan an efficient route using terrain association or dead reckoning. We covered both of these in chapter 5.

- Now that you have the fundamental steps, here is the secret to doing wilderness navigation well: Do those steps over and over again until it becomes second nature.

The preceding four steps are obviously not the whole of what you need to know, but they do form the foundation of doing land navigation well in that context. Here are a few other helpful hints that will help you during the Special Forces Assessment and Selection process:

- Listen to the rules the instructor cadres give you and do not break them.

- Although it will seem time-consuming, stop and plot checkpoints while en route to your destination. This serves as a quality control so you do not have to waste time retracing some, or all, of your route.

- Always keep up with your pace count. Keep in mind that if you draw a line and determine a distance using the map, your actual distance walked will be farther than what the map suggests. Straight-line distance on a map does not take the terrain features into consideration.

- Always check your declination and utilize it when navigating (we covered this in chapter 1).

Last but certainly not least, let's cover a vital piece of information for law-enforcement personnel specifically. As we have stated, we have had many opportunities to train and train alongside law-enforcement officers on the federal, state and local levels. Like many things in law enforcement, land navigation is one of those tools in the tactical "toolbox" that does not get used often. Thus, there is not a lot of training or dedicated standard operating procedures in the law-enforcement world in regard to navigation. Here are a few points of consideration pertaining to law enforcement:

- Write down the different agencies that you are likely to work with. Determine what coordinate system each of them works with. If you find that different agencies are on different systems, that is something administration should be aware of. For example, if a sheriff's deputy is on the scene of a motor vehicle accident and attempting to offer coordinates to dispatch, those coordinates should match up to what the responding emergency medical service uses.

- Discuss with your dispatch centers how they determine coordinates and locations. An officer's mobile data terminal can readily give coordinates to dispatch; but if that officer is in need of assistance, it is imperative that the coordinate systems match across agencies.

- Ensure the paper maps that are kept at headquarters or mobile operations centers have the same datum set. Remember from chapter 1 that if mobile units are utilizing an updated WGS 84 system and an old map is utilizing NAD 27, then the variance can be nearly 330 feet (100 m) in some instances. This variance is not that significant when you are trying to locate a vehicle with flashing lights, but it is an entirely different story if you're trying to find a fellow officer who is down. Accuracy on such things could be a lifesaver.

- Please be aware that most aircraft, both fixed-wing and rotary, utilize latitude and longitude. Most units on the ground utilize UTM, USNG or MGRS, and which system is used is completely dependent on administrative choice. Therefore, it may become necessary for units on the ground to convert units from one system to another. There are apps and websites called grid converters, coordinate converters and grid system converters that convert coordinates from system to system. These make it very easy to convert coordinates. Another "backdoor" method involves using a GPS and following these steps:

  - Enter a waypoint into your GPS and give it an easily recognizable name. That coordinate is then saved. You can think of it as figuratively putting a pin in that location of the earth. It is saved using the coordinate system that you have set in your unit as default. Let's assume that your default is UTM.

  - Go into your settings and change the coordinate system that is displayed to the other system that you need to communicate to another agency or unit (for example, Lat/Long).

  - Go to the waypoint you set in the first step. That waypoint is the same exact location but will now display with a different coordinate system.

  - This way of converting coordinates is something you should practice before you need it. It is also something your dispatch should know how to do as well.

Our military friends have more experience on such things as various topography maps, compasses and land navigation than do most law-enforcement officers, simply because of the environment in which military personnel work. A simple question law-enforcement personnel should ask is, "Who assists in landing aircraft in our area of operations?" Whoever that is most likely has good training on land navigation needs. If you see that aerial assistance is something that dispatchers or mobile units need, then that person should contact the person in your department or agency responsible for landing aircraft. This will serve to begin the conversation about a better understanding of land navigation needs within your specific agency or unit.

Now that we have spent some time on the "high-speed, low-drag" side of things, let's tone it down a bit. In the next chapter, we assist anyone desiring to teach youth groups about navigation.

WILDERNESS NAVIGATION AT NIGHT

We do not recommend that the typical recreational wilderness enthusiast navigate at night. Military and civilian first responders, however, must navigate at night when duty requires. It is our opinion that a lensatic compass is a better piece of equipment than the baseplate for such endeavors. We also believe that the United States Marine Corps is good at teaching nighttime navigation. This is how they recommend setting up your compass and navigating with it at night.

SETTING THE COMPASS FOR NIGHT LAND NAVIGATION

1. Rotate the bezel ring until the luminous line is over the fixed black index line.

2. Find the desired azimuth and divide it by 3. The result is the number of clicks that you have to rotate the bezel ring. Remember that the bezel ring contains 3-degree intervals (clicks). Sometimes the desired azimuth is not exactly divisible by 3, causing an option of rounding up or rounding down. If the azimuth is rounded up, this causes an increase in the value of the azimuth, and the object is to be found on the left. If the azimuth is rounded down, this causes a decrease in the value of the azimuth and the object is to be found on the right.

3. Count the desired number of clicks. If the desired azimuth is smaller than 180 degrees, divide the desired azimuth by 3 to obtain the number of clicks. Then count the number of clicks on the bezel ring in a counterclockwise direction. For example, let's say the desired azimuth is 51 degrees: 51 ÷ 3 = 17 clicks counterclockwise. If the desired azimuth is larger than 180 degrees, subtract the number of degrees from 360 and divide by 3 to obtain the number of clicks. Count them in a clockwise direction. For example, let's say the desired azimuth is 330 degrees: 360 - 330 = 30 ÷ 3 = 10 clicks clockwise.

(continued)

FOLLOWING A COMPASS DURING NIGHT LAND NAVIGATION

1. With the compass preset as described in the preceding section, assume a center-hold technique and rotate your body until the north-seeking arrow is aligned with the luminous line on the bezel. Then proceed forward in the direction of the front cover's luminous dots, which are aligned with the fixed black index line containing the azimuth.

2. When the compass is being used in darkness, an initial azimuth should be set while light is still available if possible. With the initial azimuth as a base, any other azimuth that is a multiple of 3 can be established through the clicking feature of the bezel ring.

QUESTIONS FOR PRACTICE

1. What is the number one rule of gun safety that applies to those who are armed and doing wilderness navigation?

2. Use the enclosed map to answer the following question: If you are tracking a suspect traveling east in Buck Creek Hollow, is there any way that the suspect could flee utilizing a vehicle?

3. Would the top of Chestnut Cliffs be a good spot for overwatch if you were providing safety for a team traveling down Leatherwood Creek Road?

4. Use the map provided to answer the following question: Would it be accurate to say that the only viable water source for deer in this area is Cave Run Lake?

5. If you wanted to travel into the areas depicted on the enclosed map by boat, where could you go to get away from areas with lots of human encroachment?

6. If you look on the enclosed map, you will find the words Chestnut Cliffs; northeast of those words is a + sign. Is that an important landmark?

7. If you wanted to see more area of the lake to the east (which is not seen on the map enclosed), which topo map would you get from the USGS?

8. A pilot relays to you that there is an important topo feature to check out at the following coordinates: 83°35'00', 38°02'30". What do you find there?

9. Use the map provided for the following question: If you had permission to hunt deer in only Bath County, Kentucky, and you parked your car at the intersection of Clear Creek and Glady Hollow roads, would you have more area to hunt to the northwest or southeast of your parking spot?

10. Would the area between Alum Knob and Hickory Hollow be better for fishing or hunting?

Answers: (1) Assume all weapons are loaded at all times. **(2)** They could not flee in a wheeled vehicle, but with assistance they could be picked up by a boat. **(3)** It appears so, but that would depend on the vegetation, the details of which a map cannot provide. **(4)** No. There are multiple small and large streams deer could drink from. **(5)** Buck Creek Hollow has no roads leading into it; the other hollows have roads. **(6)** No. It is the intersection point for the Lat/Long lines noted on the bottom and side of the map. **(7)** Olympia. Look at the graphic near the bottom right of the legend that shows the adjoining quadrangles. **(8)** It is another Lat/Long + sign located at the junction of Clear Creek and Leatherwood Roads. **(9)** Northwest, as this area is all Bath County. **(10)** Fishing. Go southeast and you run into the Menifee County line very quickly.

CHAPTER 11

TIPS AND TRICKS TO HELP SCOUTS AND FAMILIES LEARN WILDERNESS NAVIGATION

A Scout is clean . . . but not afraid to get dirty. —Mike Rowe

In June 2005, eleven-year-old Brennan Hawkins went on a camping and hiking trip with fourteen hundred other Boy Scouts in the very rugged Uinta Mountains. Not far into the trip, he became separated from his group and subsequently lost.

Brennan spent four days in the wilderness alone, surviving by drinking from creeks and eating edible plants. During that time, Brennan actually saw searchers looking for him from horseback. As many children are, he was afraid of them because they were strangers. He purposely avoided them and hid so they could not see him.

After four days, Brennan just happened to wander onto a road, where a searcher, who was on foot, saw him. He quickly made contact with Brennan, gave him some food and water and got other assistance on the way to their position.

Brennan's story is short and simple, but it illustrates many points you should consider when working with youths. Some of them are directly related to wilderness navigation, while others are pertinent in a more indirect way. Please observe the following guidelines when you train young people in wilderness navigation:

- Train all children how to hug a tree when they get lost (see page 155).

- Explain to children the difference between strangers and searchers. Tell them that searchers will look official and will often be yelling their name.

- Utilize the fundamental methods taught in this chapter to teach the children under your care. It is not clear why the young man in our opening story got separated, but something as simple as teaching an azimuth and a back azimuth can assist a child in venturing into the wilderness and returning safely.

- If you are responsible for children in a wilderness setting, you should develop the buddy system of travel in which no one goes anywhere alone. This will serve to keep youths from separating from the larger group.

There are a wide range of activities you can utilize with youths and adults who are new to wilderness navigation. In this chapter, we want to discuss some hints, competitions and games that will aid you in passing these skills on to those you are responsible to teach, mentor or train. We will examine five topics in this chapter:

- Scouting requirements

- Competitive orienteering

- Geocaching

- Wilderness navigation games

- Family activities at home

HOW TO REMEMBER THE CARDINAL DIRECTIONS

One of the first things required of young people in scouts (and also in geography class in school) is to know the four cardinal directions in clockwise order. There are several mnemonics out there to help kids remember them. I like to use "Never Eat Sour Watermelon" in our classes. We have also heard "Never Eat Soggy Waffles." Mnemonics help kids, and some adults, remember the proper ordering of the cardinal directions.

SCOUTING REQUIREMENTS

When we speak of scouts, what we are referring to is any youth who is in a program for scouting, including any of the well-known programs (such as Boy Scouts, Girl Scouts, Trail Life USA and others). The sort of training we will be covering in this section will be good for any youth group that you may be responsible for. It can be used by school teachers, church groups or sports teams as a way of building confidence and teamwork. There is rarely a land navigation class that we teach that does not have one or two active or former scouts

Image 80: Wilderness navigation is a great way for parents, teachers and scout leaders to enjoy time afield with those under their guidance.

or scout leaders in it. Scout leaders are salt-of-the-earth people. They volunteer their time and spend a lot of their own money to help train kids in a wide range of skills. Many of these skills exist outside of the leaders'. We have assisted countless scout groups in earning their survival, orienteering and tracking merit badges. Since these skills often lay outside of their leaders' wheelhouses of abilities, we are more than happy to help them bridge the gap in understanding.

Scout groups usually refer to wilderness navigation skills as orienteering. To us, orienteering is a competitive sport (and a fun one at that). We will cover orienteering later in this chapter (see page 248). For now, we need to understand that what most scout programs call orienteering is what we have been referring to as wilderness navigation throughout this book. As we often say, we are not strict about the name. As long as you can actually do the skills, we're happy.

243

For a first-ever instructional module of training for young and old alike, there are several things you will need to make it a worthwhile endeavor:

- **Tools and time:** Dedicate some class time to discussing and showing compasses, maps and other tools you may want to include (refer to chapter 4).

- **Visuals:** A whiteboard in a classroom (or a portable one for the field) will be beneficial to help train the participants. Power-Point presentations are great too. If, however, you really want to get the skills into the minds of the

Image 81a: A cattle ear tag provides a weather-proof land navigation course marker.

participants, it serves you and them better if you ask that they take notes. Writing things down and physically sketching items always help imprint them into the brain.

- **Markers:** You will need some markers for points the students are to navigate to. If you will be using a piece of property on a regular basis, a cheap way of doing this is to use cattle ear tags (see image 81a). You can mark the area and leave the markers up for the next class. If you are temporarily using a property, then engineering flagging or flags are items that you can easily pull up and use again.

- **GPS:** A GPS is important for you, the instructor, to have when setting up a course. You can mark waypoints (see page 85) so you can transfer the coordinates to your online mapping (such as sartopo.com) or software (such as Gaia or DeLorme).

- **Compasses:** You will need a compass for each participant. If that is not affordable, then purchase one for every two participants. If you want the group members to purchase their own compasses, specify exactly which compass you want them to get. If you do not do this, participants will come to the course with many makes and models, and you will have to lead the class using terminology for each of those compasses. Suunto makes a great instructional compass kit that contains thirty student compasses and a large display compass (see image 81b) for the instructor to use. This makes it easier for the instructor to show things in front of a group.

Image 81b: The large teaching compass, next to a regular student compass, provides an instructor with a great visual tool in a classroom setting.

ACTIVE TRAINING

We took a look at the various merit badge requirements for different scouting organizations. We have broken them down into ten requirements that all programs seem to offer. The following list is a good benchmark for all scouting programs and other related programming for youth:

- Cover fundamentals of safety for the area that you will be navigating in. This will include the most likely injuries (e.g., a twisted ankle), wildlife issues and how to best deal with them if they are encountered, poisonous plants (e.g., poison ivy) and what to do if someone gets lost. As we discussed in chapter 5 (and in Craig's book *Extreme Wilderness Survival*), if someone gets lost, the best course of action is to have them sit down and wait for help to arrive. Make sure that you tell the children that if they get momentarily lost, that they will not get in trouble. Also instruct them that if their name is called they should answer back.

- Address terminology with the students. Discuss the definition of orienteering and list alternative terms they may have heard, such as wilderness navigation, map and compass skill, map reading and more.

- Show the participants a topographic map (refer to chapter 1). So that participants do not get confused with too much information, the principles of map reading should be boiled down like so:

  - Explain the various colors on the map and what each color represents.

  - Explain how to measure distances utilizing the scale of the map. Demonstrate how to use the edge of a compass, a string or a ruler to transfer measurements to the scale of the map. It is best to use very prominent features on the map to do this. A road or trail intersection to the edge of a waterway is one example.

  - Show how to orient the map with the compass.

  - Discuss grid lines on the map and how to find coordinates.

  - If the group is ready for it, dig into the topic of declination. If not, bypass it for now and have them do some coursework and then add declination a little later. Please note that we are not saying that declination is not important. It most certainly is. From experience, we have discovered that it is a huge stumbling block for many. That is why we are recommending you bring it into the puzzle later.

- Show the participants how a compass works (refer to chapter 2). So that participants do not get confused with too much information, the principles of using a compass should be boiled down like so:

  - Explain how to properly hold a compass.

  - Point out the north-seeking arrow.

  - Explain the four cardinal directions and what degree amount is associated with each.

  - Demonstrate how to do Red Fred in the Shed and explain what it means.

- Set up a known 330-foot (100-m) distance on a level surface for getting participants' pace counts. Explain to the students that it is not a competition. They must walk naturally. For competitive children, we recommend making this exercise a silent one where they do not talk. Have them walk the 330 feet (100 m) a minimum of two times and write down their number each time. This way, they (and you) can get an average pace count. If you allow participants to talk, they will often try to match numbers to be like their friends or take more steps to get a higher number, thinking it is a competition.

- Set up a small course (five points minimum) with points in an open field. The distance between the points at this level should be 330 feet (100 m) or less. The points need to be visible from one to the next. This will assist students in going from point to point and setting the correct azimuth on their compasses. You can give them these readings to begin with. Use the same course and go from a different route. Since they can see the next point, have them take a bearing with their compass and write it down.

- Have an in-depth discussion after everyone has had time to go through the course. Answer questions as they come and take time to point out the things you observed while leading the course.

- Set up another small course that has waypoints in cover (such as a wooded area). The students will have to leapfrog with a partner or use items on the terrain to keep them online. Remind them to keep up with their pace count.

- Have assistants on each of the points to aid beginners in finding the locations as students come to them. Radio contact with the assistants and those you are teaching is very beneficial to this. Through preplanning, the students should know that if they get lost, they need to stop and sit down. They could use a radio or cell phone to tell you.

- Have the students continue this type of coursework until you are satisfied with their performance. As their abilities increase, increase the distance between the points. Also, you might want to introduce obstacles for participants to navigate around.

AFTER-ACTION REVIEW

An after-action review is imperative for increasing the participants' skill sets. With children, this will involve asking questions, such as the following:

- What part of the course did you like the most?

- What part of the course did you like the least?

- What did you find difficult to do while practicing?

- What sort of equipment would you like to have to make it easier?

More than anything, asking the preceding questions serves you in procuring information to help the students get better at the practice. If you get an opportunity to hear their thoughts, you know what items you as an instructor can improve on. Don't take this work lightly. This sort of training could literally lead those under your care to save their own lives or the lives of others someday.

COMPETITIVE ORIENTEERING

When we use the term competitive orienteering, we want to distinguish this from orienteering in general. Orienteering is a competitive sport in which you put wilderness navigation skills into practice. In many circles, the word orienteering has come to mean navigation with map and compass. It may just be semantics, but we believe it is important to distinguish the two.

Originally, orienteering was developed by the militaries of Scandinavian countries to enhance land navigation skills for their soldiers. Orienteering made its way to the United

Image 82: Orienteering courses will often have highly visible signage and designators.

States in the early 1940s. Orienteering is a great way to take your wilderness navigation skills up a level or two—maybe even three.

There are orienteering clubs throughout the world and they get together periodically to test their skills. Most of these competitions will feature courses that are designed for beginners as well as advanced navigators. At its heart, a competitive orienteering event is a race to see who can use a map and compass to orient their way through a course. At each of the points (called controls) that have been plotted, there are either devices to punch your personal card or receive some sort of token that you take with you. This proves to the competition staff that you made it to each point. The goal of the competition is to make it through the entire course with the fastest time. Here are a few things that are worthy to note when it comes to orienteering:

- Once you begin doing these competitions, view them as races with yourself only. Your goal should be to finish the course efficiently, not necessarily quickly. This means getting to all your control points as directly as possible.

- Note the scale of the map when you receive it. Most orienteering maps are 1:10000 scale, which is a much smaller scale than your typical 1:24000 USGS quad maps.

- Some orienteering race maps will have areas in the topography that detail the density of vegetation along the routes. If you are competing with others, this should be a strategic consideration.

- Your pace count is vital to this sort of competition. Most competitors will run a course rather than walk it. By having a good pace count (regardless of the topography and whether you are walking or running), you will probably come upon your control point more efficiently.

Now that orienteering as a sport has been around for a few decades you can find various races that involve more specialized interests, such as high-mountain and cross-country skiing, mountain biking and even tactical scenarios. The last type of race will involve control points in which competitors shoot or do physical fitness challenges along the way. We have assisted in courses such as these for federal law-enforcement officers.

GEOCACHING

Geocaching is a wonderfully fun way to use your GPS unit (whether a dedicated unit or a phone app) to practice your navigation skills. Geocaching involves hunting for and finding hidden objects utilizing GPS coordinates that you obtain from a website (geocaching .com). You can download or manually enter the data into your GPS receiver. Alternatively, you can easily download the Geocaching® App (available for both iOS and Android). The reason I suggest utilizing your GPS is because to play the geocaching game, you will need to put in lots of waypoints then

Image 83: Most geocaches are camouflages but hold fun trinkets. Don't forget to log your visit.

utilize the GPS to navigate to them. Most navigation occurs by car rather than foot travel. By utilizing your GPS to geocache, you get very familiar with your unit's functions and learn how to utilize it effectively. With that said, if you just want to geocache for the fun of seeing what the caches have for you, then please download the app. The caches come in many shapes and sizes. Many are located in ammo boxes or hardy plastic containers to withstand the elements. What you find in these caches will be detailed in a moment.

When you start geocaching, you will find many things that surprise you. If this is the first time you have heard of geocaching, please know there are caches all around you. These caches contain gifts and trinkets of interest. There are official caches put out by tourism folks, but typically the most fun ones are put out by other geocachers. Here are a few tips that will help you have a safe and positive geocaching experience:

- Most of the cache location coordinates are simple and easy to plug in. As you find more caches and gain experience, you can dig into the coordinates that are obtained by ciphers or secret codes.

- Many of the locations contain a logbook and pencil, which you can use to prove that you stopped at the location. Others have trinkets that you trade. Visit a few with trinkets so you can get a feel for the types of items people leave. Once you see the typical trinket, you can gather a few goodies to take and trade yourself.

- The caches are supposed to be left in such a way that your typical passersby do not notice them. This can sometimes mean they are hidden in areas with little to no foot travel, or they are cleverly disguised. My family once spent two hours searching and knew we were within 1 foot (30 cm) of the cache. We made a fun family memory that day.

- Once you find a hiding spot, move away quickly with the box to examine, log or trade some contents. Staying at the exact location for an extended time will bring too much attention to the spot.

- When trading trinkets, always leave the cache better than you found it. Don't take a nice trinket and leave a wad of chewed gum—that ruins the fun.

- There are some special trinkets called travel bugs. These are not items you keep. Your job is to move them so they make their way around the world. By keeping up with a particular travel bug on the Geocaching website you can see how far it has traveled.

We hope this discussion on geocaching generates enough interest for you to get started. It is a good, honest way to both have fun and develop your GPS skills.

GEOCACHING ACRONYMS

Another fun aspect to geocaching is the use of acronyms in logbooks. Acronyms are used so that if non-geocachers find the cache, they cannot break the fun secret code. Here are the top ten acronyms used:

1. **BYOP (Bring Your Own Pen):** This means there is no writing instrument at the cache site.

2. **CITO (Cache in Trash Out):** This acronym is a reminder to keep the outdoors better than you found it.

3. **DNF (Did Not Find):** Posted to the website to let other geocachers know you did not find the cache.

4. **FTF (First to Find):** It's a big honor to be the first to find a newly placed cache.

5. **LPC (Lamppost Cache):** This indicates a common cache found on or in a lamppost.

6. **SWAG (Stuff We All Get):** This term refers to trinkets and trade items.

7. **TB (Travel Bug):** This acronym refers to trackable trinkets.

8. **TFTC (Thanks for the Cache):** This is a courteous response to finding a fun cache.

9. **TNLN (Took Nothing. Left Nothing.):** This is an acronym informing others that you just visited the cache.

10. **TOTT (Tools of the Trade):** This term refers to tools you might need to find or retrieve a cache.

WILDERNESS NAVIGATION GAMES

Sometimes wilderness navigation can get very dry for those that don't have a *need* to learn the skill but only *want* to learn. Since it is such a vital skill to have for wilderness adventuring, we like to meet people where they are. Following is a list of games that Nature Reliance School has utilized in school programs and for scouting groups to make the practice a bit more fun. We are certain you can find some way to adapt the following to yourself or the groups you adventure with:

- **Blindfold bearing and back bearing (image 84):** Set out five markers, for five participants, about 10 feet (3 m) apart in an area where the participants can walk one hundred paces. Give the compasses to the participants with any heading you choose. The participants then put something over their eyes, such as a blindfold or paper bag, in such a way that they cannot see in front of them but can look down at their compass. They then walk one hundred paces on their setting and determine the back heading. After walking one hundred paces on the right azimuth, they should arrive back to their marker. If you want to award prizes for fun games, then award them for the people who arrive closest to their marker.

- **Bearing relay:** This is a fun game for teams. Have a topographic map for each of the teams. Make a central point on each of the maps and call it Camp, Home or something similar. Fill out easily recognizable features on the map. When you say, "Go," one of the team members gets a card, goes to the map and determines the bearing from the central point to the map feature on the card. After they determine the bearing, they record it and the next person in line does the same thing. You will need cards for each member of the teams.

Image 84: A blindfold-bearing and back-bearing exercise allows the student to develop a good pace count and only allows them to see the compass but no surroundings.

253

As the instructor, you should have a listing of the actual degrees they should have found. Add up all the amounts where their readings differed from the actual. The one with the lowest amount wins.

- **Nature hunt:** We often do a variation of this exercise in our regular land navigation exercises. In this one, you set up a normal land navigation course with various waypoints. You can make it as easy or as difficult as the skill levels of those in attendance allow. At each of the waypoints, the participants will need to identify a tree or plant. This helps the participants be aware of different tree species instead of just viewing the points as a part of the exercise. You can also have a treasure hunt along the way. We did this once with a bunch of high-speed military veterans, and they had a blast. It may seem like a silly game, but this exercise teaches one of the most important aspects of wilderness navigation—the ability to navigate and have good situational awareness at the same time. We most often do this with our youth programs. Some activities you can have participants pursue along the way are:

  - finding a nut of any kind

  - finding a piece of dead bark from a tree (they must be able to identify the tree)

  - snapping a picture of any wildlife they see

  - finding a rock they find interesting

FAMILY ACTIVITIES AT HOME

We utilize the following methods regularly to teach children how to apply the cardinal directions to their daily lives. These are good ways to bridge the gap for those who have no understanding of direction—in other words, these activities apply direction finding to things most people already know. Some of these family activities are obvious, others not so much. We teach many things in a very fundamental way. To those used to wilderness navigation, fundamental instruction may seem too obvious. Our experience tells us this is not so for those without any exposure to wilderness navigation or even sound teaching in geography. Even some young adults in high school don't recognize that the sun rises in the east and sets in the west.

Do you know someone who has an incredible "sense of direction"? More often than not, that person simply pays attention to their surroundings. A good sense of direction is something that can be developed over time. Think about the early humans for a moment. Don't you believe that when they obtained, utilized or created some sort of structure to live in that at some point they recognized where the sun came up and went down? Most likely, they realized that the sun played a role in keeping them alive through heat management.

You, too, can learn to recognize where the sun rises and sets, and you should know the four cardinal directions as they relate to your home. One practical way of doing this is to print the letters for each of the cardinal directions in large font, using one sheet of paper for each direction: N for north on one piece of paper and so on. You can then use your compass to place the four letters on the walls inside your home (preferably in the room you spend the most time in). By keeping these letters up on the wall, you will have a regular reminder of where the four cardinal directions are.

If you take the time to observe nature as it relates to these directions, you can gather important information without the need for any wilderness navigation equipment. Here are some items you will notice. Some of the following are obvious, others are not so obvious:

- Remember that the sun comes up in the east and sets in the west. Having this knowledge can help you warm your house during the cold months. Open any blinds that are primarily in the southern sky to let the most sunlight in during daylight hours. This simple method can save you money on your heating bill.

- Recognize where the prevailing winds are. You will note that one portion of your house gets the most wind, rain, snow and so on. You can plant trees on that side of your house to break some of those winds. Those winds will have a drastic effect on your energy bills.

- Recognize that the north side of your house will get less sunlight. It is on that side you can harvest or otherwise use plant species that do not need full sunlight.

- If you are interested in disaster preparedness, you should note several important points on a map of the area surrounding your home. Mark on the map the directions to go for safety, for secondary shelter and for water. Knowing the directions to leave your home under the stress of disaster is an important aspect of planning for such events.

To further enhance your family's involvement, including kids, you can regularly ask them or yourself questions such as the following:

- In which direction is the grocery store located?

- In which direction is the school located?

- Is our backyard north of the house?

The preceding are simple ways to get yourself and those you live with to think in terms of directions listed as north, south, east or west rather than left or right. While that may not seem important, it most certainly is. By adjusting the terms in which you think, you will start developing a better sense of direction.

We hope this chapter has given you more creative ways to go about honing or maintaining your wilderness navigation skills. Wilderness navigation is a perishable, "use it or lose it" skill. You may be motivated by your need to have these skills; but if you're like many of us, you don't need them as much as others. We want to have them on the rare occasion that we will need them. The games and methods in this chapter will help you do exactly that.

QUESTIONS FOR PRACTICE

1. What is the number one rule when teaching wilderness skills to youths?

2. What is the most likely injury for anyone in a wilderness area? How do you help prevent this injury while teaching wilderness navigation to young people?

3. What is the most common word used by scout groups for wilderness navigation?

4. Should you teach declination to youths?

5. What are two mnemonics you can use to help students remember the four cardinal directions?

6. What is one rule that youths should follow when you are helping them with pace count?

7. What is a good distance between points for beginners studying wilderness navigation?

8. What is one question that you can ask after a wilderness navigation course is practiced with youths?

9. What is one primary difference between competitive orienteering maps and regular USGS topo maps?

10. What does the geocaching acronym TNLN stand for?

Answers: (1) Make it fun—don't expect them to behave like adults. (2) Twisted or broken ankle. Teach them to have good situational awareness and pay attention to where they are walking. (3) Orienteering. (4) It will depend on how skilled the group is. If they are answering all the questions and exercises you give them, then dig into declination. If they are having trouble with the basics, do not. (5) "Never Eat Sour Watermelon"; "Never Eat Soggy Waffles." (6) They should not talk during the practice—they will automatically compete and not get an accurate pace count. (7) 330 feet (100 m). (8) "What part of the course did you like the most?"; "What part of the course did you like the least?"; "What did you find difficult to do while practicing?"; "What sort of equipment would you like to have to make it easier?" (9) The scale is typically 1:10000. (10) Took Nothing, Left Nothing.

CONCLUSION

THE TEN COMMANDMENTS OF WILDERNESS NAVIGATION

We shall not cease from exploration
And the end of all our exploring
Will be to arrive where we started
And know the place for the first time.
—T.S. Eliot

Every portion of this book was written for you to become a new or better wilderness navigator. It is all important. We do recognize that in the modern world, a concise methodology is beneficial to those with little time. With that in mind, we want to remind you of the top ten things you must do to be a safe, successful and efficient wilderness navigator:

1. Orient your map to the terrain in front of you. This is the first step to integrating the tools that you take with you. Utilize your compass (or natural navigation methods) to find north. Then hold your map or lay it down in such a way that it corresponds to north as well.

2. Monitor your position regularly. If you are using a map, keep it close and accessible. You can then check your position on it regularly and efficiently. You should also know your direction of travel at all times. This does not mean you get out your compass and take a heading every ten minutes. It does mean that you should make a mental note as you check your map for your direction.

3. Maintain your situational awareness. Do not be so focused on the map that you miss the things that are around you. The purpose is twofold: The first is to be able to recognize landmarks of importance for navigation purposes, and the second is to enjoy the outdoors.

4. Each time you contact a notable terrain feature, mark it on your map for confirmation. This includes places such as stream crossings, a trail split, a notable cliff face or changes in vegetation (e.g., from forested wilderness to opening).

5. Keep a logbook or running tally on your personal maps. This is rarely done by most, but we can assure you that it will increase your wilderness navigation skills exponentially. At each notable point or feature, note the degrees turned, the distance traveled and the time. This is a great item to review once you make camp or after you get home. It will help you educate yourself on the measurable aspects of wilderness navigation.

6. Keep a running tally of your distance walked through these estimations, through pace count or through both.

7. On occasion and for good reason, stop and take in the surroundings. Use the opportunity to practice natural navigation as a quality-assurance measure.

8. When traveling distances longer than 330 feet (100 m), assume—despite all your positive efforts—that you will be slightly off. When getting close to your destination, look in 360 degrees.

9. Your destination may still be in front of you, but it may also be left, right or behind you because you walked past it.

10. Anytime you have a "gut feeling" about your position, direction or distance, use your knowledge and skill to confirm or negate it. Although a sense of direction can definitely be developed, it should be a small part of your wilderness navigation skill set. Utilize the skills you learn and practice to replace gut feelings with facts from your compass, your maps and the environment.

It is exciting when we get to the end of a book. It is always our intent to write for the sake of you, the reader. We imagine that along the way you have read and practiced the skills we've discussed. You most likely have a good compass and a map or two with a waterproof case. We hope you have completed a fair amount of on-trail terrain association and have at some point gone off-trail (where allowed) to test your map and compass skills. You probably kicked up a leaf or two, maybe broke a branch to mark your way. If you have done some or all of those things, this book is a success. If not . . . what are you waiting for? Get out there, because we hope to see you on or off the trail!

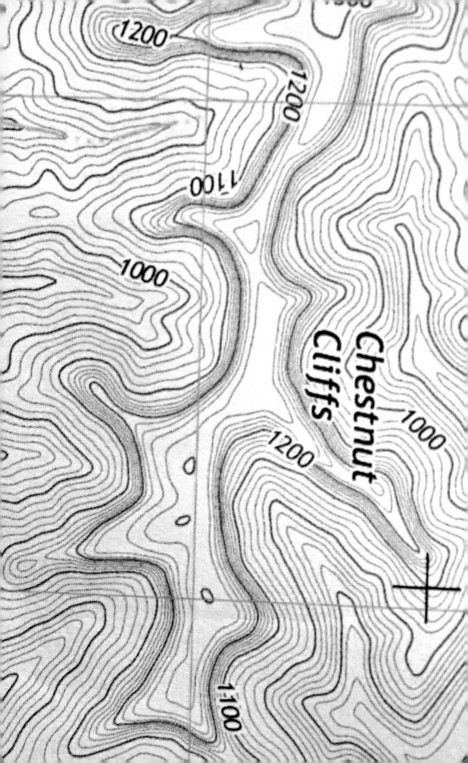

APPENDIX: TOPOGRAPHIC MAP SYMBOLS

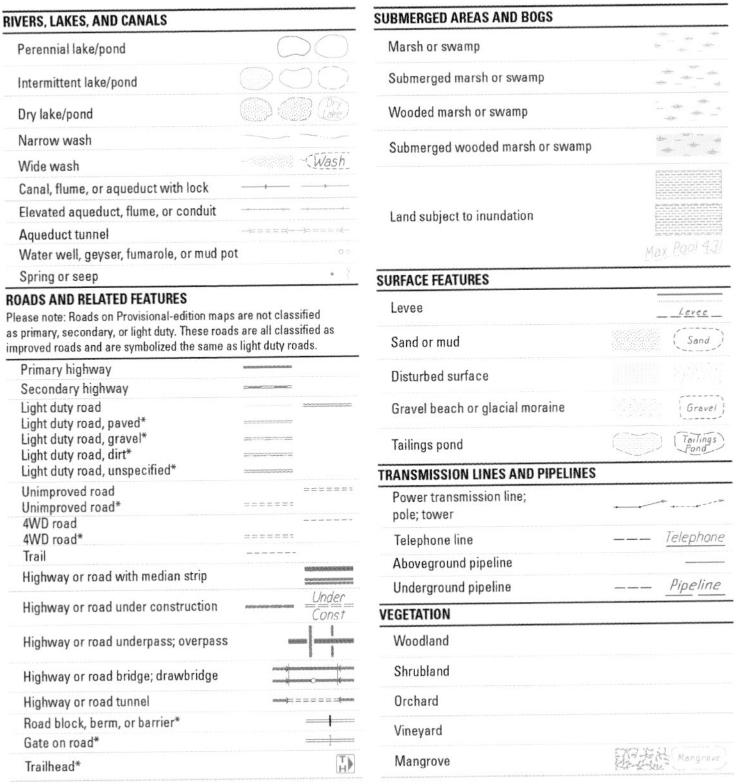

RIVERS, LAKES, AND CANALS

Perennial lake/pond	
Intermittent lake/pond	
Dry lake/pond	
Narrow wash	
Wide wash	Wash
Canal, flume, or aqueduct with lock	
Elevated aqueduct, flume, or conduit	
Aqueduct tunnel	
Water well, geyser, fumarole, or mud pot	
Spring or seep	

ROADS AND RELATED FEATURES

Please note: Roads on Provisional-edition maps are not classified as primary, secondary, or light duty. These roads are all classified as improved roads and are symbolized the same as light duty roads.

Primary highway	
Secondary highway	
Light duty road	
Light duty road, paved*	
Light duty road, gravel*	
Light duty road, dirt*	
Light duty road, unspecified*	
Unimproved road	
Unimproved road*	
4WD road	
4WD road*	
Trail	
Highway or road with median strip	
Highway or road under construction	Under Const
Highway or road underpass; overpass	
Highway or road bridge; drawbridge	
Highway or road tunnel	
Road block, berm, or barrier*	
Gate on road*	
Trailhead*	

SUBMERGED AREAS AND BOGS

Marsh or swamp	
Submerged marsh or swamp	
Wooded marsh or swamp	
Submerged wooded marsh or swamp	
Land subject to inundation	Max Pool 4.3

SURFACE FEATURES

Levee	Levee
Sand or mud	Sand
Disturbed surface	
Gravel beach or glacial moraine	Gravel
Tailings pond	Tailings Pond

TRANSMISSION LINES AND PIPELINES

Power transmission line; pole; tower	
Telephone line	Telephone
Aboveground pipeline	
Underground pipeline	Pipeline

VEGETATION

Woodland	
Shrubland	
Orchard	
Vineyard	
Mangrove	Mangrove

Image 85: USGS top coloration and symbology.

CONTROL DATA AND MONUMENTS

Vertical control

Third-order or better elevation, with tablet	BM × 5280
Third-order or better elevation, recoverable mark, no tablet	× 528
Bench mark coincident with found section corner	BM + 5280
Spot elevation	× 7523

GLACIERS AND PERMANENT SNOWFIELDS

Contours and limits	
Formlines	
Glacial advance	
Glacial retreat	

LAND SURVEYS

Public land survey system

Range or Township line	
Location approximate	
Location doubtful	
Protracted	
Protracted (AK 1:63,360-scale)	
Range or Township labels	R1E T2N R3W T4S
Section line	
Location approximate	
Location doubtful	
Protracted	
Protracted (AK 1:63,360-scale)	
Section numbers	1 - 36 1 - 36
Found section corner	—+—
Found closing corner	—+—
Witness corner	WC +—
Meander corner	—◄ MC
Weak corner*	—+—

Other land surveys

Range or Township line	
Section line	
Land grant, mining claim, donation land claim, or tract	
Land grant, homestead, mineral, or other special survey monument	▫
Fence or field lines	

MARINE SHORELINES

Shoreline	
Apparent (edge of vegetation)***	
Indefinite or unsurveyed	

MINES AND CAVES

Quarry or open pit mine	✕
Gravel, sand, clay, or borrow pit	✕
Mine tunnel or cave entrance	◄
Mine shaft	▪
Prospect	x
Tailings	Tailings
Mine dump	
Former disposal site or mine	

PROJECTION AND GRIDS

Neatline	39°15' / 90°37'30"
Graticule tick	55'
Graticule intersection	+
Datum shift tick	—+—

State plane coordinate systems

Primary zone tick	640 000 FEET
Secondary zone tick	247 500 METERS
Tertiary zone tick	260 000 FEET
Quaternary zone tick	98 500 METERS
Quintary zone tick	320 000 FEET

Universal transverse metcator grid

UTM grid (full grid)	273
UTM grid ticks*	269

RAILROADS AND RELATED FEATURES

Standard guage railroad, single track	
Standard guage railroad, multiple track	
Narrow guage railroad, single track	
Narrow guage railroad, multiple track	
Railroad siding	
Railroad in highway	
Railroad in road	
Railroad in light duty road*	
Railroad underpass; overpass	
Railroad bridge; drawbridge	
Railroad tunnel	
Railroad yard	
Railroad turntable; roundhouse	

RIVERS, LAKES, AND CANALS

Perennial stream	
Perennial river	
Intermittent stream	
Intermittent river	
Disappearing stream	
Falls, small	
Falls, large	
Rapids, small	
Rapids, large	
Masonry dam	
Dam with lock	
Dam carrying road	

BATHYMETRIC FEATURES

Area exposed at mean low tide; sounding datum line***	
Channel***	=====
Sunken rock***	

BOUNDARIES

National	
State or territorial	
County or equivalent	
Civil township or equivalent	
Incorporated city or equivalent	
Federally administered park, reservation, or monument (external)	
Federally administered park, reservation, or monument (internal)	
State forest, park, reservation, or monument and large county park	
Forest Service administrative area*	
Forest Service ranger district*	
National Forest System land status, Forest Service lands*	
National Forest System land status, non-Forest Service lands*	
Small park (county or city)	

BUILDINGS AND RELATED FEATURES

Building	
School; house of worship	
Athletic field	
Built-up area	
Forest headquarters*	
Ranger district office*	
Guard station or work center*	
Racetrack or raceway	
Airport, paved landing strip, runway, taxiway, or apron	
Unpaved landing strip	
Well (other than water), windmill or wind generator	
Tanks	
Covered reservoir	
Gaging station	
Located or landmark object (feature as labeled)	
Boat ramp or boat access*	
Roadside park or rest area	
Picnic area	
Campground	
Winter recreation area*	
Cemetery	Cem

COASTAL FEATURES

Foreshore flat	Mud
Coral or rock reef	Reef
Rock, bare or awash; dangerous to navigation	
Group of rocks, bare or awash	
Exposed wreck	
Depth curve; sounding	18 23
Breakwater, pier, jetty, or wharf	
Seawall	
Oil or gas well; platform	

CONTOURS

Topographic

Index	6000
Approximate or indefinite	
Intermediate	
Approximate or indefinite	
Supplementary	
Depression	
Cut	
Fill	
Continental divide	

Bathymetric

Index***	
Intermediate***	
Index primary***	
Primary***	
Supplementary***	

CONTROL DATA AND MONUMENTS

Principal point**	3-20
U.S. mineral or location monument	USMM 438
River mileage marker	Mile 69

Boundary monument

Third-order or better elevation, with tablet	BM 9134 BM 277
Third-order or better elevation, recoverable mark, no tablet	5628
With number and elevation	67 4567

Horizontal control

Third-order or better, permanent mark	Neace Neace
With third-order or better elevation	BM 52 Pike BM393
With checked spot elevation	1012
Coincident with found section corner	Cactus Cactus
Unmonumented**	

APPENDIX: SUGGESTED RESOURCES

Maps		
SARTopo	sartopo.com	Website used by many SAR teams.
Google Maps	google.com/maps	You can purchase additional layers to use with Google Maps.
National Geographic	nationalgeographic.com/maps	Software and folded, waterproof maps.
USGS Store	store.usgs.gov	Request printed maps or download and print yourself.
Army Corps of Engineers	www.usace.army.mil/Library	Rivers, lakes and other waterways.
National Park Service	nps.gov	Maps and brochures detailed for each national park in the US.
US Forest Service	www.fs.fed.us	Maps covering all national forests.
outrageGIS mapping	outragegis.com	Unique and enjoyable topo maps and trail profiles.
Appalachian Trail Conservancy	appalachiantrail.org	Resources specific to the Appalachian Trail.
Pacific Crest Trail Association	pcta.org	Resources specific to the Pacific Crest Trail.
Sheltowee Trace Association	sheltoweetrace.org	Resources for the greatest trail in the United States.
National Resources Canada	nrcan.gc.ca	Topographic maps of Canada.

Compasses		
Cammenga	cammenga.com	Military-grade lensatic compasses.
Suunto	suunto.com	Brand preferred by Nature Reliance School.
Brunton	brunton.com	Quality compasses with unique features.
Silva	silva.se	Compasses developed for orienteering.
GPS Receivers		
DeLorme	delorme.com	Company recently purchased by Garmin; many DeLorme products still available.
Garmin	garmin.com	High-quality GPS receivers and sports-specific watches.
Lowrance	lowrance.com	Marine and fishing electronics.
Magellan	magellangps.com	Off-road navigators.
Trimble	trimble.com	Geospatial and industrial GPS technologies.
Books		
Be Expert with Map & Compass (3rd ed.)	Björn Kjellström and Carina Kjellström Elgin	Focused on the sport and practice of orienteering.
The Natural Navigator	Tristan Gooley	Covers in-depth natural navigation.
The Essential Wilderness Navigator	David Seidman and Paul Cleveland	Focused on international backpacking and hiking.
Land Navigation Handbook	Marine Barracks (Washington, DC)	Course manual for land navigation needs of the US Marines.
The Green Beret's Compass Course	Don Paul	Insight into methods and ways of US Special Forces selection.
Extreme Wilderness Survival	Craig Caudill	Covers mind-set, skills, tactics and gear for wilderness survival.
Ultimate Wilderness Gear	Craig Caudill	Covers the efficient purchase, use and maintenance of wilderness gear.

ACKNOWLEDGMENTS

Flip through the book again. It looks good and fits nicely in the hand, doesn't it? Many thanks to Page Street Publishing for that. We wrote the words, took the pictures and created the graphs. Page Street does the hard work of putting it all together and, along with Macmillan Publishers, gets it out to you, the reader. Rob Brandt of Watchbell has done another amazing job with his illustrations to help clarify difficult-to-understand points. Nichole Kraft of Paper Weight Editing has once again demonstrated great patience, skill and communication as the copyeditor for this project.

Many thanks to the nearly countless students of Nature Reliance School who have joined us in the woods and around the campfire for classes in wilderness navigation and so much more. We have learned as much from you as you have from us. Many of the challenges and questions you have had are the foundation of this book. Our students are a true melting pot of people. Thank you for entrusting us with your wilderness education.

Tracy is sending out a hearty thanks to the United States Army Reserve for introducing him to land navigation. It was that education that built a foundation for him to teach land navigation at Nature Reliance School. Teaching forced him to dig deep and improve his skill set. Tracy also thanks the search-and-rescue teams of Wolfe and Menifee Counties. It is by serving others in those teams that Tracy has been able to practically apply what he knows about wilderness navigation. Last and certainly not least, Tracy wants to thank his wife, Samantha, for her continued support while he is away teaching, training and searching for others.

I would like to say a huge thanks to Tracy. Without him, I would not have an effective and efficient wilderness navigation skill set, nor would this book have been written. I would also like to thank my family, who endured the writing of this, my third book. This book required years of practicing and testing methods and theories to prove them right or wrong. It also required a grueling writing process to get it right. When I was in my own head and writing too much, my family (Jennifer, Lily and Zane) knew the right time to pull me away and go to the woods for the fun of it. I love you all—and thank you!

Lastly, we want to thank you, the reader. Thank you for purchasing this book and supporting all our endeavors at Nature Reliance School. We would not, and could not, do it without you. Now enjoy what the wilderness has to offer!

ABOUT THE AUTHORS

Craig Caudill is the founder and director of Nature Reliance School in Kentucky. He is the author of *Extreme Wilderness Survival* and *Ultimate Wilderness Gear*. He has also written for *Backwoods Survival Guide*, *Wilderness Way*, *Ballistic* magazine, *Self Reliance Illustrated*, *American Frontiersman* and *American Survival Guide*, and he pens a weekly newspaper column for the *Winchester Sun*. Craig actively teaches backcountry and wilderness skills to military, federal, state and local law-enforcement, emergency medical and search-and-rescue teams. He has taught survival and wilderness navigation skills to biology and wildlife students from fourteen different Southeastern universities. He has been a featured guest on public educational television as well as numerous news segments, podcasts and magazine interviews. He has an incredibly active blog, YouTube channel and social media presence, through which he offers free wilderness skills. Follow his work at naturereliance.org.

Tracy Trimble is one of the lead instructors at Nature Reliance School and has been involved since its inception in 2006. Tracy developed an appreciation for all things outdoors by exploring, hiking, biking and horseback riding in the wilds of Kentucky. He was first introduced to land navigation in the United States Army Reserve, where he served six years in various capacities on the M1 Abrams tank and later as a drill sergeant. Tracy leads all wilderness navigation courses for Nature Reliance School, which attracts students developing their skill sets for use in the government and public sectors. Tracy is an active member of two search-and-rescue teams and the local fire department, where he utilizes wilderness navigation and other backcountry skills to bring others to safety.

INDEX